DETHRONING THE
QUEEN *of*
HEAVEN

DETHRONING THE
QUEEN *of*
HEAVEN

*Cancel this Demon's Ancient Agenda to
Destroy Your Life and Control Nations*

REBECCA GREENWOOD

DESTINY IMAGE® PUBLISHERS, INC.

P.O. Box 310, Shippensburg, PA 17257-0310

"Publishing cutting-edge prophetic resources to supernaturally empower the body of Christ"

This book and all other Destiny Image and Destiny Image Fiction books are available at Christian bookstores and distributors worldwide.

For more information on foreign distributors, call 717-532-3040.

Reach us on the Internet: www.destinyimage.com.

ISBN 13 TP: 978-0-7684-7469-5

ISBN 13 eBook: 978-0-7684-7470-1

ISBN 13 Hardcover: 978-0-7684-7472-5

ISBN 13 Large Print: 978-0-7684-7471-8

For Worldwide Distribution, Printed in the U.S.A.

1 2 3 4 5 6 7 8 / 28 27 26 25 24

ACKNOWLEDGMENTS

As I sit here in the early hours of the morning upon completing the final chapter of this book, I must take the time to honor special family and friends. I know it is said that a book project would not be possible without the help of others. With my past writing projects I would say that this has been true. But not as much as it has been with this writing assignment. I can truthfully say that this book has been the most challenging and intense project to date. Of course, the subject matter, Dethroning the Queen of Heaven, would greatly contribute to this factor. I strongly felt that this message must be done with such excellence. Not that the past writing endeavors did not have that same motivation. This subject matter required thorough and in-depth research. I have known this information for many years and as you will discover, this manuscript is packed full of history. Much of which required the locating of citations, ensuring facts are current and correct. This has taken hours of dedicated time and a team to make all this possible.

First, I want to thank my husband, Greg. The hours of reading all that has been written. The wisdom to ensure that all the necessary details and strategic pieces of history have been included. The hours that you have given such grace because of the time this project required. The words of encouragement during the times I was tired, when your support and belief in me and this message was the exact thing I needed to keep going. And most of all your love and prayers. I love you, dear. Thank you, from the bottom of my heart.

To my precious daughter Kendall, who has worked hours reviewing and editing the chapters of the book. Your sweet messages of, "Momma, this is good! Don't take a word out," imparted such a beautiful faith to keep writing through to completion. You are such a beautiful woman, wife, daughter, sister, auntie, and most importantly a lover of Jesus and dynamic prayer warrior. Thank you, sweet one, for your help. I could not have done this without you! I love you.

To all my family, Rebeca, Justin, Katie, Mark, Kendall, Kole, and precious Emmy Grace, Hazel Faith, and Jubilee Mae. Thank you for your patience and your awesome support. For all that you do, the help you give, and the time you pour into what He has called us to do. You all are the joy of our lives. We are proud of each of you. You are all so loved and cherished. I am blessed to be your Mom and Lolli. I love you all more than words can express.

To Robyn Weatherman. Thank you, dear one, for your hours of research. The assistance in writing the prayers. The phone calls of allowing me to process and your amazing servant's heart. I know this final week of completing this book that you also have not slept because of your passion and heart to help ensure things were done in excellence. I am beyond grateful. You are so cherished and loved.

To Anthony Turner and Brandon Larson. Your contributions are priceless! Thank you for your yes to write the chapters and share your in-depth spiritual insight, great research, revelation, and wisdom. Many will be set free and prayer warriors greatly empowered to see cities, regions, spheres of influence changed and transformed. I'm beyond grateful.

To our intercessors. Becky Albert, Brenda Bechtel, Robyn Weatherman, April Farris, Cindy Dravenstott, Lonnie Lavender, Denise Nutt, Melanie Taylor, Ruthann McDonald, Dee Dee Roberts, Regenia Pounds. Thank you! Your prayers and intercession carried me through to the finish line! I love you all so very much.

To SPAN, Strategic Prayer Apostolic Network. You are an amazing, dedicated, on-fire band of prophetic warriors. Greg and I love running this race with you. I'm so proud of each of you. What miraculous breakthroughs and victories have been realized through your yes to the blueprint strategies from heaven. Spheres of influence, cities, regions, nations have all experienced His victorious redemption in your obedience to Him. History belongs to the intercessor and you are history makers. I love you!

To Eddie and Alice Smith. Thank you for seeing the calling and destiny on our lives and bringing us under your wings. You have poured in, mentored, awakened, challenged, celebrated, and loved us so well. Thank you for teaching us holiness, how to walk on fire for Him, how to be abandoned worshippers, how to enter beyond the veil and live a life of a surrendered yes in that abiding place. Thank you for teaching us how to live bold for Him and for imparting into me and pulling out of me the prophetic warrior I am called to be. We love you!

Mike and Cindy Jacobs, thank you for pioneering the prayer movement and releasing the clarion call for this new era—that we are called and chosen to bring healing to the nations.

Possessing the Gates of the Enemy forever impacted me. Thank you for paying the price and pioneering the way for women, prophets, apostles, and those called to be world changers. Thank you for standing by us, praying for us, challenging us, and believing in us. Cindy, thank you for being the apostolic prophetic Momma to so many. I am so beyond honored to have you in my life. We love you both.

To Chuck Pierce. Thank you for always welcoming us to host our annual prayer gathering at Glory of Zion. Thank you for honoring Peter and Doris so well. Thank you for your generosity. For all the prophetic words over the years that literally thrust us into our new season. For leading the way with the prophetic call to raise up the triumphant reserve. For your tireless pioneering work in the nations and our nation. For paving the way for so many. I want to express a sincere thank you. We love you.

Ché Ahn, thank you for your words of encouragement. Thank you for the love and the support you have given us. I'm so blessed to be a core faculty member for Wagner University and to continue to speak and impart to so many who are called to be world changers. Thank you for always being available and there for us when we need you and for being a great leader and father to so many. We love you.

To Peter and Doris Wagner, where do I even begin. While I know Peter is in heaven, I have to say thank you to such a great man of God and father in the faith. Doris, Greg and I so dearly love you and Peter. For all the years we have known each other and run together, we are beyond blessed and grateful. Thank you for the belief you and Peter have had in us and all you have imparted to and instilled in us. We are fruit, the next generation, of all the pioneering work you have done throughout the nations. What an honor to have been raised up in the amazing prayer movement that you ignited and led, which has changed nations. Your dedication and resolute yes has changed the lives of countless people and greatly impacted nations. Thank you for the apostolic pioneering to rally, convene, activate, mobilize, commission, and send out the intercessors, believers, and leaders to engage in strategic-level spiritual warfare prayer to see principalities conquered, a harvest awakened, and transformation realized. I will never forget in 2007, the first time Peter challenged me to write a book on the Queen of Heaven. I finally did it! Woohoo! We now have *Confronting the Queen of Heaven, The Queen's Domain,* and *Dethroning the Queen of Heaven.* Doris, I pray that this book honors the teaching and legacy that you and Peter pioneered. We love you.

Finally, I want to say thank You, Jesus. Thank You for Your saving grace. The victorious deliverance You have brought into my life. The magnificent truth of Your Word. For the glorious encounters in intercession and knowing You more. Thank You for the beautiful privilege to be called as an intercessor, prophet, and spiritual warrior to the nations. I love You, Jesus.

CONTENTS

Introduction 1

Chapter One   Who Is This Queen of Heaven? 11

Chapter Two   Come Out from Her. 27

Chapter Three   Called and Chosen to Conquer. 57

Chapter Four   Ishtar. 73

Chapter Five   Lilith. 103

Chapter Six   Isis. 131

Chapter Seven   Jezebel. 159

Chapter Eight   Mami Wata. 183

Chapter Nine   The Knights Templar 201

Chapter Ten   Santa Muerte 227

Chapter Eleven   Checkmate 259

Notes. 275

INTRODUCTION

Why a book on the topic of the Queen of Heaven? This is a great and valid question that I would like to address up front. The year was 1994. The Lord was leading me in season of night watch intercession, waking me on a regular basis from midnight to 3:00 am to intercede for our nation and the nations. One evening, I had a deep and profound encounter with Jesus in which a spiritual understanding and journey began, engaging against and conquering the Queen of Heaven principality and her demonic army of darkness. That night, He began to direct me to passages in the Word of God that highlighted and named the ancient demonic entity, the Queen of Heaven. The two scriptures (which will be explained further in Chapter One) that He initially directed me to are found in Jeremiah.

> *The children gather wood, and the fathers kindle the fire, and the women knead the dough, to make cakes to the queen of heaven, and to pour out drink-offerings unto other gods, that they may provoke me to anger* (Jeremiah 7:18 ASV).

Then all the men who knew that their wives were burning sacrifices to other gods, and all the women who were standing by, a large group, including all the people who were living in Pathros in the land of Egypt, answered Jeremiah, saying, "As for the word (message) that you have spoken to us in the name of the Lord, we are not going to listen to you. But rather we will certainly perform every word of the vows we have made: to burn sacrifices to the queen of heaven (Ishtar) and to pour out drink offerings to her, just as we ourselves and our forefathers, our kings and our princes did in the cities of Judah and in the streets of Jerusalem; for [then] we had plenty of food and were prosperous and saw no misfortune" (Jeremiah 44:15-17 AMP).

I believe oftentimes we read the Word and do not fully study to gain understanding of what is being shared and the spiritual significance that we should be grasping and applying in our beliefs, lives, and culture. It seems this is greatly the case when it involves ancient cultures. Even though we glean great spiritual insight and life from His Word, there can be a tendency to dismiss spiritual realities spoken of due to the fact they feel so far removed. For me, in this encounter, I knew it was Holy Spirit leading me to scriptures that spoke about Ishtar, Ashtoreth, Astarte, Artemis, Diana, Innana, and others. At that point in time, I would not have been familiar with scripture references about this principality. As I heard Him speak the references to turn to in my Bible, it would be another instance in which a mention was made to the Queen of Heaven or one of her many adaptations.

As I continued on the Spirit-led journey, I began to scripturally research the origins of these evil demonic entities and gods. Who are these ancient entities and principalities that were being worshipped and specifically addressed by name in the Word of God? How were they worshipped? Why were these evil and demonic spirits worshipped? How did these principalities keep people and regions bound in darkness? The further I dove into research in Bible commentaries and all the historical and archeological findings of these entities, I soon discovered they were all a part of the Queen of Heaven demonic structure—same spirit in operation but different names, adaptations, and manifestations. It grew increasingly clear that this demonic entity, the Queen of Heaven, in many adaptations has demonically inserted and infiltrated her evil influence and grip in cultures, banking systems, witchcraft/occult practices, abortion/killing of the younger generation, racism and slavery, occult secret societies, sexual perversion, seduction, homosexuality, trafficking of bodies and souls of people. She has for centuries influenced many forms of arts and entertainment and religion and spiritual practices, some of which have infiltrated the Church. Scripture clearly states that the Lord abhors the worship of this demonic principality, as stated in Jeremiah 44:20-23 (AMP):

> *Then Jeremiah said to all the people, to the men and*
> *to the women and to all the people who had given him*
> *that answer, "The smoking sacrifices (incense) that you*

burned in the cities of Judah and in the streets of Jerusalem—you and your forefathers, your kings and your princes, and the people of the land—did not the Lord remember [in detail your idolatry] and did it not all come into His mind? The Lord could no longer endure it, because of the evil of your acts and the repulsive acts which you have committed; because of them your land has become a ruin, an object of horror and a curse, without inhabitant, as it is this day. Because you have burned sacrifices [to idols] and because you have sinned against the Lord and have not obeyed the voice of the Lord or walked in His law and in His statutes and in His testimonies, therefore this tragedy has fallen on you, as it has this day."

As I began to inquire further of the Lord as to why He was leading me into this understanding, He spoke to me, "You will be used in your nation and the nations to deal with this demonic entity." To speak honestly, at that time I was not overly excited about what I had heard. What would this look like and how would this unfold? Now, having arrived at over 34 years of experience in deliverance ministry and ministering and praying strategically in over 48 nations, I can honestly state that we have seen many individuals set free from the demonic influence and grip of one of the many adaptations of this entity. And we have seen great breakthrough and victories in the spheres of influence, cities, regions, and nations that we have been assigned to by the Lord in order to bind and dethrone this principality.

Some might be pondering the following thought. In ancient history these demonic entities were worshipped, but are they really in operation today? And why is this understanding necessary for me to know? Allow me to share a recent and blatant gathering that involved the intentional worship and welcoming in of *Lilit,* also known as *Lilith,* one of the many manifestations of the Queen of Heaven. Its purpose—to grip families, specifically the younger generation, and to encourage the conjuring up of, welcoming in, and establishing of relationship with the demon. The following was taken directly from the website of the Minnesota Art Museum where the ritual occurred.

> At August Free First Saturday, Brooklyn-based artist Tamar Ettun (she/they) will present Lilit the Empathic Demon. The performance is inspired by Lilit, an aerial spirit demon with origins in Sumerian, Akkadian, and Judaic mythology. Families are invited to create a vessel to trap the demon that knows them best—perhaps the "demon of overthinking"—and then participate in a playful ceremony to summon and befriend their demon. Demons have a bad reputation, but maybe we're just not very good at getting to know them. Do you have a demon that creeps into your thoughts? Maybe the "demon of overthinking" or "the demon of not trusting your gut"? Work with visiting artist Tamar Ettun to design a vessel for holding the demon you know best!
>
> After designing your trap, Lilit the Empathic Demon will come from the dark side of the moon to lead you in

locating your feelings using ancient Babylonian techniques. This collective and playful demon summoning session will conclude with a somatic movement meditation, designed to help you befriend your shadows.[1]

I am sure many of you feel a great and righteous indignation and anger when reading about this totally depraved and evil agenda to demonically capture and hold individuals, families, and our young in its evil grip. I know I do!

I do teach much of this information in our deliverance school and ministry training and also in the CHI Regional Transformation Spiritual Warfare School.[2] I must confess, I have put off over and over again the writing of this manuscript because I understand and realize the price for calling out, identifying, completely uncovering, and confronting these spirits. There will be many who do not appreciate the message in this book, but there will be even more who are grateful to be informed and equipped to see these satanic spirits and principalities uncovered, defeated, destroyed, and dethroned.

I also want to state that I and those who partner with us in our calling to strategic intercession place our intimate relationship with our Heavenly Father, Jesus, and Holy Spirit first and foremost. We spend time in glory-anointed worship, in His throne room presence beyond the veil in intercession for revival and awakening for our nation and the nations. This is our highest calling. We are ones who cry out and who have surrendered to glory-anointed intercession for revival and a harvest of souls. And from His glory we are ones who say yes to advancing as prophetic warriors to see strongholds and principalities defeated to usher in and secure awakening and transformation. It is not either-or, but both-and. For in-depth teaching discussing intimacy with Him, His glory presence, and encounters that empower victorious warfare strategies, my book *Glory Warfare: How the Presence of God Empowers You to Destroy Works of Darkness* is a resource to help awaken this calling and journey.

I will speak more in-depth of a very recent glory encounter in intercession in Chapter One, but I will state briefly that in this time of intercession He clearly spoke that the demonic battle that is raging is reaching a climax with a victorious showdown between the Church and the Queen of Heaven. In the Book of Revelation, John was taken into—or as some translations state "caught up"—in a profound heavenly encounter in which he experienced many glorious and wondrous moments and was shown what would take place in times to come. Some of this involved prophetic sight into intense and fateful events and also the victorious spiritual warfare engagement between the Kingdom of our Heavenly Father and satan's kingdom of darkness. In this divine encounter he is clearly shown the harlot, sometimes interpreted as Babylon, the mother of prostitutes. After vividly describing her and her evil activity and influence in Revelation 17. John scribes several key focuses, which I will briefly highlight before our deep dive into the message unfolded in this book.

John scribes the Lord's directive to His people and the seven churches, which we will discuss in-depth in Chapter Two, *"The one whose heart is open let him listen carefully to what the Spirit is saying now to all the churches. To the one who overcomes*" (Revelation 2:7 TPT).

The angel revealed to John the judgment of this great prostitute, the whore of Babylon, a manifestation of the Queen of Heaven, "*Come, and I will show you the judgment of the great prostitute who sits enthroned on many waters*" (Revelation 17:1 TPT).

The angel spoke to John that He and His chosen ones will conquer, "*They will wage war against the Lamb, but the Lamb will conquer them, for he is Lord of lords and King of kings! Those who are with him will also conquer them, and they are called 'chosen ones' and 'faithful ones'*" (Revelation 17:14 TPT).

John heard a voice making this clarion call and declaration, "*My people come out from her so that you don't participate in her sins*" (Revelation 18:4 TPT).

John is shown her destruction and the declaration to rejoice, "*Rejoice over her, O heaven, you apostles and prophets and holy believers, rejoice! For on your behalf God pronounced the judgment against her that she wanted to bring on you*" (Revelation 18:20 TPT)!

Wow! So impactful are these declarations and promises, all of which will be discussed thoroughly on the journey we are about to embark on. Truly, I find this is also my cry and my prayer. As this message is released, we will all see any place we have aligned with this demonic spirit and receive deliverance, freedom, and healing so that we will have ears to hear what the Spirit is saying and we will be empowered to overcome and conquer. For this very reason, this book is different. I absolutely do not believe we are to focus on darkness and evil all the time. The Lord and His Word are our steadfast and constant focus. That being said, the teachings of the different manifestations and the brief history lesson given through time will give us better understanding with which we can also apply prophetic revelation and insight. The two together provide a strategic map and plan to engage in informed, victorious intercession to see transformational breakthrough realized.

For many years, prayer warriors have been praying for this nation and the nations. And all of us have witnessed the Lord move in magnificent breakthrough and victories. I personally want to express my sincere gratitude and speak honor to all of you amazing prayer warriors. It is also my prayer and belief that we, the army of our Heavenly Father, will be empowered to see further equipping, spiritual sight, and revelation to what has always been hidden in plain sight. That this will not be read and treated as revelation for knowledge's sake, but an empowering word, a sword of the Spirit, of victorious insight and strategy to see this principality's grip broken and its hold over spheres of influence, culture, and nations uprooted, thrown down, defeated, and conquered.

Chapter One

WHO IS THIS QUEEN OF HEAVEN?

Who is this Queen of Heaven? As stated in the introduction, Holy Spirit began to speak to me about this principality and her many manifestations in 1994, from which there has been continued growth in spiritual revelation concerning how this spirit establishes its satanic grip in culture. Great understanding through research has been gained and wisdom on how to see her and her evil agendas dethroned.

I'm going to bring us into a journey of discussing different manifestations of the Queen of Heaven that are active throughout the world. It would be very easy to fill up entire books with each of these forms of this demonic principality. To help us all have a clear idea of the big picture on the ways the Queen of Heaven operates, however, the chapters in this book focus on brief, overview histories of each of the principality's forms. This will give us all a more high-level understanding, especially for those who are new to teaching on this topic.

Be aware: we cannot talk about demonic principalities without going through hard history. I wish I could make these things feel better, but I can't. What my contributors and I tell in this book is what has happened in and throughout history. This is the reason for the many testimonies shared throughout the book—to champion the beautiful and glorious and victorious redemption that occurs from our Heavenly Father, Jesus, and Holy Spirit when we choose to no longer tolerate and ignore these principalities but address them as what they really are in the authority of Jesus! This journey we are on together in this book will begin with a recent and profound prophetic encounter that occurred in August 2023, when Jesus clearly revealed the Queen of Heaven's evil agendas through history and time and in which He decreed His dominion mandate and divine intent to see the principality dethroned from her demonic seat over people and nations. Let's begin.

I and a team made up of ten prophetic worshippers and intercessory prayer warriors were in a deep place of glory intercession for the nations. Suddenly, I was taken up in an encounter in the throne room of Jesus. While seeing Him, my gaze completely focused on Him, a vision began to unfold like a movie reel. He took me to and through significant moments of time when the demonic entity, the Queen of Heaven, was empowered and established throughout history and nations. As Jesus was speaking to me in this divine face-to-face encounter, the team was certain to capture on audio what was occurring. I began speaking aloud what I heard Him clearly and repeatedly state and pose as a revelatory question in every historic moment that He revealed to me throughout time, history, and the nations: "Don't you know My battle has always been with her."

I will stop here and explain that there are many demonic principalities along with their numerous manifestations that have established their demonic grip over spheres of influence and nations. And His clarion call to us as believers has always been to conquer all satanic principalities. In this encounter, it was as if He was specifically highlighting this Queen of Heaven principality because now is the time to see her schemes uprooted, plundered, defeated, and destroyed. He was speaking in a manner that will be forever etched in our hearts and alive in our spirits as we continue to advance in the days ahead. And as previously stated, this is an assignment the Lord has given to us and our prayer network for many years.

As the vision continued, He spoke, "Don't you know that the Ekklesia's battle is with her." I saw how the Queen of Heaven established herself at the tower of Babel, in Egypt, in Rome, in Turkey, in Israel, Europe, many nations within Europe, in Asia, in Africa, in Mexico, and in other nations and spheres of influence. How she has established herself in North America. I began to weep and repent for every place we in our bloodlines have agreed and aligned with this principality and ways the Church has aligned and come into agreement with her. I wept and repented concerning many ways that cultures have aligned and agreed with this evil entity. I then found myself in a deep prophetic declaration, "Come out from her! Come out from her!"

Following this weighty encounter and momentous vision, He led me and the prophetic intercessory team to open the Word and read Revelation 17, 18, and 19. I must admit I have read and studied the Book of Revelation many times. But as I read through John's revelation in the midst of Holy Spirit's manifest glory that was still strong, evident, and tangible, the words in those passages jumped off the page in a depth of revelation, wisdom, and understanding that I had not experienced before when reading John's supernatural and heavenly encounter.

Our Battle Is Against Principalities, Powers, Rulers of Darkness

To begin the study of this ancient principality, it is necessary to initiate this discussion on the foundation of understanding against whom our spiritual battle is. Paul gives a clear description of satan's army in Ephesians 6:12, *"For we do not wrestle against flesh and blood, but against principalities, against powers, against the rulers of the darkness of this age, against spiritual hosts of wickedness in the heavenly places"* (NKJV). Let's take a moment and define these descriptive terms to ensure we are all in the same vein of understanding. The Greek word for *principality* is *arche*. It means *chief magistrate or ruler that originates from the beginning* (Strong's #G746). The word for *authorities* is *exuosia*. It means "superhuman, delegated influence, jurisdiction" (Strong's #G1849). *Kosmokrator* is the Greek word for demon gods, and it refers to world rulers under satan (Strong's #G2888). This word was often used to refer to a conjuring of pagan deities or supreme powers of darkness mentioned in occult rituals. *Poneria* is the word for evil spirits. It refers to maliciousness, iniquity, vicious, degenerate, sinful, dark spirits who are possessors of this dark world (Strong's #G4189). The scripture makes it clear that our battle is not with each other but should be aimed in the spirit realm and directed toward satan and his hierarchy of rulers and demons.

Other names frequently used for *principality* are *territorial* or *master spirit*. These evil spirits are assigned to geographical territories and social networks. Their assignment is to keep large numbers of humans—networked through cities, neighborhoods, regions, nations, people groups, industries, government, businesses, education systems, religious alliances, media, or any other form of social institution—in spiritual captivity. Results of this oppression include but are not limited to the rampant injustice, oppression, perversion, misery, hunger, disease, natural disasters, racism, human trafficking, economic greed, wars, and the like now plaguing our world. So let's begin our discovery and discussion of this Queen of Heaven, this *arche* demonic principality, that has been established in culture from ancient times and one that we are still dealing with throughout cultures in our world today.

JEREMIAH IDENTIFIES HER BY NAME

Then all the men who knew that their wives were burning sacrifices to other gods, and all the women who were standing by, a large group, including all the people who were living in Pathros in the land of Egypt, answered Jeremiah, saying, "As for the word (message) that you have spoken to us in the name of the Lord, we are not going to listen to you. But rather we will certainly perform every word of the vows we have made: to burn sacrifices to the queen of heaven (Ishtar) and to pour out drink offerings to her, just as we ourselves and our forefathers, our kings and our princes did in the cities of Judah and in the streets of Jerusalem; for [then] we had plenty of food and were prosperous and saw no misfortune. But since we stopped burning sacrifices to the queen of heaven and pouring out drink offerings to her, we have lacked everything and have been consumed by the sword and by famine." And said the wives, "When we were burning sacrifices to the queen of heaven and were pouring out drink offerings to her, was it without [the knowledge and approval of] our husbands that we made cakes [in the shape of a star] to represent her and pour out drink offerings to her?" (Jeremiah 44:15-19 AMP)

The Hebrew word for Queen of Heaven used in the above scripture is *meleket*. It is defined as "a female royal ruler, one who is a governmental head of a kingdom" (Strong's #H4446). It stems from the Hebrew word *malak*, defined "to reign and to descend to the throne" (Strong's #H4427). In this scripture, it is specifically referring to a pagan deity who rules in the heavens, meaning the area of the stars, skies, air, as a region above the earth including the horizon. She is an ancient principality also known as the moon goddess that has been worshipped in many forms with many different names, which I term *adaptations* or *manifestations*. For some I will give in-depth explanation in the chapters of this book. Here is a brief overview of various names for this entity: Ishtar, Astarte, Diana, Artemis, Sophia, Cybele, Minerva, Lilith, Jezebel, Venus, Ashtoreth, Isis, Juno, Medusa, Santa Muerte, Mami Wata.

Peter Wagner states in his book *Confronting the Queen of Heaven*, "The Queen of Heaven is the demonic principality who is most responsible under Satan for keeping unbelievers in spiritual darkness."[1] Even though this quote was coined by Peter in

1998, I have to honestly admit that I still believe this to be true today and in this time and season.

This is a goddess system or structure of worship originating in the most ancient cultures in history. Most of them engaged in a polytheistic worship structure, meaning they revered and bowed to multiple gods. The worship would often focus on a male god or principality. In some cultures, the male god could be viewed as the moon god, but most often he was portrayed as the sun god. It is important to understand that even cultures in which the sun god was revered, it was the rotation or cycle of the moon that had the "life-giving" significance and superiority. Why? Because it was linked with the cycles of the female body. Therefore, the moon was the source of blood flow and fertility. And as will be discovered as you continue to read, many forms of the Queen of Heaven would appear in the form of a male or female.

It is sometimes found that the male god controls harvest, wealth, and grain, and the female god controls fertility, idolatry, and family well-being. In some beliefs, such as the Egyptian deification of Osiris and Isis that is still perpetuated in freemasonry and eastern star, she possessed the power through witchcraft to bring resurrection life. Therefore, Osiris, the Egyptian adaptation of the sun god, when killed twice had no power to raise himself from the dead. It was Isis who carried the powers of witchcraft and divination to resurrect Osiris—not once, but twice. Which brings us to the conclusion, that in this structure she is the principality with the ultimate power. It places and positions her with more authority in the structure of freemasonry than that of Osiris, who is known in this secret society as the adaptation of Baal, the sun god. All of this will be explained in-depth in Chapter Six.

The Queen of Heaven in her many manifestations was also recognized as the goddess of war who exerted ultimate control over the agriculture of the world. In these cultures, the belief was that prosperity and blessing was linked with their loyal, abandoned worship and devotion to her. She maintained her grip through the demonic forces linked to her hierarchal structure.

If she was not worshipped and appeased then people would experience war, poverty, confusion, and chaos. Barrenness and poverty would be other exacting blows this entity would deliver to those who tried to break free from her evil and demonic control. Through fear, this principality has governed cultures. I find one of the most disturbing comments made by the people in response to the Word of the Lord through Jeremiah in the above scripture, *"As for the word (message) that you have spoken to us in the name of the Lord, **we are not going to listen to you**"* (Jeremiah 44:16 AMP, emphasis mine). Those devoted to her worship refused to listen to or hear the prophetic Word of the Lord through Jeremiah. She vexes the spirit man and hardens the hearts, minds, and souls of her followers, hindering the willingness or ability to respond to the prophetic word of the Lord and to the Lord Himself. As a result, she keeps a strong grasp as a world ruler on wealth structures of influence, religious structures, industries, governments, regions, nations, and sadly even some within the Church.

THE GREAT PROSTITUTE

Then one of the seven angels who had the seven bowls came and spoke with me, saying, "Come here, I will show you the judgment and doom of the great prostitute who is seated on many waters [influencing nations], she with whom the kings of the earth have committed acts of immorality, and the inhabitants of the earth have become intoxicated with the wine of her immorality." And the angel carried me away in the Spirit into a wilderness; and I saw a woman sitting on a scarlet beast that was entirely covered with blasphemous names, having seven heads and ten horns. The woman was dressed in purple and scarlet, and adorned with gold, precious stones and pearls, [and she was] holding in her hand a gold cup full of the abominations and the filth of her [sexual] immorality. And on her forehead a name was written, a mystery: "BABYLON THE GREAT, THE MOTHER OF PROSTITUTES (false religions, heresies) AND OF THE ABOMINATIONS OF THE EARTH" (Revelation 17:1-5 AMP).

The Greek word for *prostitute* is *porne*, defined as "a woman who engages in sexual intercourse for payments, bribes, or favor" (Strong's #G4204). The Hebrew word for *great* is *gadol* (Strong's #H1419). It means "pertaining to a large quantity or a large area taking up a greater mass than normal." It signifies having a high status, one that is older than another, to be in a spatial dimension that is elevated compared to other dimensions, a high priest with special duties. This great prostitute is seated on many waters. This position of being seated signifies a mark of distinction. Throughout history, when we see those of royalty seated on a throne it signifies royal power. The same principle is true in the spiritual realm—demonic, antichrist, and satanic principalities also take seats of authority over and into culture from which they unleash evil and satanic agendas and power. In this encounter, John clearly scribes how kings and inhabitants of the earth have committed acts of immorality and inhabitants are intoxicated with her wine of seduction, perversion, and evil.

I find it interesting that Babylon is a feminine noun and is also called the Mother of prostitutes and abominations of the world. In essence, this angel is stating that Babylon is the womb, the birthing place, the Mother of the great harlot, of prostitutes and atrocities. As we will discover, Babylon is also known as a gate. To gain a clear understanding, allow me to take a few moments to teach about Babylon and Babylonia, which is referenced and spoken of in the Word of God.

ANCIENT BABYLONIA

Babylonia refers to an ancient region located in Mesopotamia, which is the area between the Tigris and Euphrates rivers in present-day Iraq. The term is derived from the city of Babylon, which was one of the most significant and influential cities in the region. The historical and cultural significance of Babylonia is closely tied to the city of Babylon and its prominence in the ancient world. The name Babylon appears in various forms in different languages.

The original Sumerian word for *Babylon* was ka-din-gir-ra KI. Ka is an ideogram meaning *gate.* Dingir is an ideogram for "god." ...*KI* is the sign for "land, earth." ...Under this linguistic scenario, the Sumerian name for *Babylon* meant "Gate of God Land." Babylon came to be pronounced "Babylon" when the Akkadians and Babylonians conquered the city in the 2nd millennium BC and gave Babylonian pronunciations to Sumerian words. The Babylonian for *gate* was babum and for *gate of* was bab. Their word for *god* was ilu—Bab ilu–Babylon.

...[The] pronunciation came into Hebrew as babel in the Hebrew Old Testament and is how we get our modern pronunciation of the word "Babylon," meaning in Akkadian/Babylonian "Gate of God."[2]

Whew! That's a mouthful! It is clear that this etymology reflects the city's spiritual and cultural importance as a center of worship and a gateway to the gods.

Babylonia was known for its advanced civilization, including achievements in architecture, astronomy, mathematics, and law. The Code of Hammurabi, one of the earliest and most complete written legal codes, originated from this region. Babylonia's historical significance extends to its role in various empires, including the Old Babylonian Empire, the Neo-Babylonian Empire (under rulers like Nebuchadnezzar II), and its interactions with neighboring civilizations, such as the Assyrians and Persians. The term *Babylonia* is commonly used by historians and scholars to refer to the larger region surrounding Babylon, encompassing various city-states and territories that were part of the broader Mesopotamian landscape.

The worship of the Queen of Heaven in ancient Babylonia was an intricate and multifaceted aspect of Mesopotamian spiritual practices. The Queen of Heaven, also known by various names such as Inanna or Ishtar, was the major goddess in the Mesopotamian pantheon located in the city of Babylon. I will explain further about Ishtar and her significance and satanic infiltration and hold in today's cultures in Chapter Four, but it will be helpful to share her role that was established in this ancient culture to signify that this high-ranking *arche* principality in satan's kingdom has impacted culture, spheres of influence, and nations for thousands of years. Here are just a few key highlights of her demonic entrenchment in this culture.

Her Attributes

The Queen of Heaven was revered as a powerful deity who embodied fertility, motherhood, and spiritual authority. She was known as the goddess of love and war. She was often depicted with symbols that highlighted her significant role as nurturer and guardian of the people and the land. She was associated with the planet Venus and was believed to embody the morning and evening star. She was revered as one who could both nurture and provide a warrior-like protection against enemies.

Ishtar, as stated, was one of the most recognized and influential representations of the Queen of Heaven in Babylonian culture. To ancient Babylonians and contemporary occultists, Ishtar was and is Babylon. She could bestow life and destruction and was often seen holding a lion, symbolizing her power and ferocity, or also with a star circlet symbolizing her celestial nature.

Cultic Practices

Her worship involved elaborate rituals and ceremonies. Dedicated temples were centers of worship and cultural activity. The tower of Babel mentioned in Genesis 11 was one of the most notable architectural feats thought to honor her among other gods. It was called the Etemenanki, in the Sumerian language meaning, "temple of the foundation of the earth."[3]

Festivals celebrating the Queen of Heaven were significant events in the Babylonian calendar. These were done in order to secure her favor and protection. Often these festivals included processions in which statues or symbols of the deity were paraded through the city. Sacrifices, incantations, prayers, and dancing would ensue. Offerings were made to her and could range from simple foods to extravagant gifts of gold and precious stones. Communal feasts occurred to strengthen social bonds and shared identity among the worshippers.

Priesthood and Temples

The priesthood played a pivotal role in her worship, acting as intermediaries between the deity and her followers. Priests and priestesses were responsible for conducting rituals, maintaining temples, and interpreting her will. Temples dedicated to the Queen of Heaven were not only places of worship but also centers of learning and cultural activities, underscoring the deity's importance in Babylonian society.

These practices highlight the complex relationship between the Babylonians and their gods, in which worship was not only a matter of personal faith but also a crucial component of social and cultural identity from the royal court to the common farmer. Through these rituals and ceremonies, the Babylonians signified that this Queen of Heaven was immersed within the natural and social order. Further, they believed that through their abandoned devotion, her favor was given for prosperity.

Her Influence on Art and Literature

Her influence greatly infiltrated art and literature through hymns, prayers, and epic poems celebrating her "great" deeds. One of the oldest known pieces of literature, *The Epic of Gilgamesh,* specifically references Ishtar's role in the Babylonian pantheon and her significant interaction with mankind in the cultural and religious landscape. And as stated above, she often was flanked by a lion or even an owl, which were symbols of her protection and wisdom. These artistic renderings not only served as spiritual icons but also as cultural symbols of the Babylonians' values and beliefs.

The Symbol of Power and Protection

She was often invoked by kings and warriors for victory in battle and also by ordinary people for protection and justice. Her temples served as sanctuaries for the oppressed where she served the role as the guardian of all social order and moral conduct. She was the one charged with maintaining balance and peace.

Her Empowerment with Political Authority

The relationship between the veneration, dedication, and worship of the Queen of Heaven and the Babylonian political authorities was evil and perverse. Kings often portrayed themselves as ones chosen by the demonic deity, which in turn legitimized their rule and divine favor. They would engage in a ritual termed the sacred marriage rite, *heiros gamos,* in which a symbolic and spiritual act of sex and union between the goddess and the mortal king transpired representing the fertility of the land.[4]

Cross-Cultural Influences

The worship of the Queen of Heaven, particularly in the form of Ishtar, shared similarities with the worship of deities in neighboring regions. Inanna in Sumerian culture was an early form of a goddess who shared many attributes with Ishtar, including aspects of love, war, and fertility. Thus highlighting the progression of the deity's worship from Sumerian to Babylonian culture. In the broader Ancient Near East, similarities can be drawn with Astarte in Canaanite religion and Aphrodite in Greek mythology, both of whom were associated with love, beauty, and fertility.

Legacy in Modern Culture

As will be explored, the Queen of Heaven's influence extends into modern culture through literature, art, worship, witchcraft, psychology, feminism, abortion, racism, banking structures, freemasonry, culture, governments, arts and entertainment, etc. The prototype of the powerful feminine deity, embodying both creation and destruction to societies, unfortunately resonates in contemporary discussions about gender, power, and spirituality. Her demonic legacy can be seen in the ongoing fascination with ancient mythologies and witchcraft within the modern-day occult belief in her as the divine.

Her worship in ancient Babylonia represents a deep-rooted and demonic relationship between her and humankind. Much like what was shown vividly to me in the prophetic encounter, through her numerous manifestations across cultures and time, this demonic entity has left an lasting mark on human civilization, illustrating her continuance in evil plots and agendas attempting to establish power, invade spiritual beliefs and practices to shape societies, inspire art and literature, and foster spiritual connections and practices among and within cultures and societies. As a result, her diabolic legacy, with its dark and demonic symbolism and cultural infiltration, continues to move forward in the evil agenda to cause intrigue and to trap people and society in her dark lies. In my research, I have read how countless have said this Queen of Heaven brings inspiration and offers insights into the shared human experience and the universal search for meaning and connection to the spiritual. This is beyond devastating for those who entertain these evil lies, but for me it also stirs a righteous anger toward her. The Word of God clearly states that Babylon, the Mother of all prostitutes and abominations, will fall! Let's continue this journey of discovery to further be equipped as His called, chosen, and faithful ones to see this principality and her satanic agenda destroyed and conquered.

Chapter Two

COME OUT FROM HER

In Revelation 18:4-5, John shares a clear, audible command that is resounded out in his divine prophetic encounter, *"And I heard another voice from heaven, saying, 'My people, come out from her so that you don't participate in her sins and have no share with her in her plagues, because her sins are heaped as high as heaven and God has remembered her vileness'"* (TPT). The Greek word for come out is *exerchomai.* It means "go, come out, pass away, to depart from, and to cease existence with" (Strong's #G1831). He then makes a declaration, "My people," which seems to be a straightforward declaration of who we are as His people—children and believers in Him. It is interesting to learn that it also carries further spiritual meaning and weight.

The term *egṓ,* which is translated "my" in this scripture, speaks of proclamations that God makes concerning Himself as the "I am," the self-witness of Jesus that He is the Messiah, the Beginning and the End, and the self-announcement that is made by those who receive salvation and become Christians. In another ancient theological use, *egṓ,* was also used in divine proclamations in the ancient Near East, Babylonian liturgy, and Egyptian papyri. One example is the hymnal prediction: "I am Isis." Isis is the Queen of Heaven out of the ancient worship of Egypt. This declaration was a point of self-representation, self-glorification, and self-commendation of this deity.[1] To paint the prophetic picture of what is occurring in this declaration of "come out from her *My* people," the Lord is declaring a warfare proclamation and command in the spiritual atmosphere that we are not to be her people; we are to completely come out of all beliefs, practices, worship, and existence with her and to fully function in and with Him as His people. It is a warfare declaration and a Kingdom of Heaven divine decree of identity that we are His! In my Becca Greenwood language of spiritual warfare, it makes me shout, "Take that, Queen of Heaven! Jesus' decree in the atmosphere is we are not yours, but His!"

Therefore, our response to this must be an abandoned, surrendered, absolute, obedient yes! We must realize the depth of surrender, purity, holiness, and fear of the Lord we are to walk in. Why? We cannot tear down what we are holding up. Therefore, we must intentionally welcome Holy Spirit, His purifying presence, and fire to show us any place in our lives that aligns with sin and deal with it. We are coming out of all existence, beliefs, practices with this Queen of Heaven structure, Babylon and Babylonia, and its hold on us personally and culturally. We absolutely ensure that there is nothing in us or our family bloodlines where we have embraced or entertained this demonic entity. We do so by repenting, renouncing, breaking its hold, and evicting it out of our lives.

There is also the truth of accepting personal responsibility for the Kingdom of Heaven inheritance that has been bestowed in and to us. I personally believe this is why John's divine encounter scribed in the Book of Revelation began with the prophetic insight concerning the seven churches—what was not pleasing and was pleasing to the Lord in those churches and what the Kingdom of Heaven promise is for those who overcome. These churches and believers lived in pagan cities, cultures, and structures. One in which many demonic principalities were entrenched in every realm of life and culture, thus greatly impacting the spiritual atmosphere and climate. Yet they were given a clarion call to be the consecrated, on fire, set apart ones who overcome. You see, as His chosen army we must be intentional to deal personally in our spiritual lives in these areas to prepare us for the calling to conquer Babylon and dethrone the Queen of Heaven. Therefore, let's take this time to learn of the seven churches and intentionally choose a spiritual walk and life that aligns and increases in the areas that please the Lord and repent for all areas of sin we find ourselves in as He challenged the seven churches. Let's then set our face like flint to be believers who have ears to hear what the Spirit is saying to the churches and walk in obedience to be the overcomers He has called us to be.

CHURCH OF EPHESUS

The Church of Ephesus was commended for their deeds and patient endurance. They did not tolerate those who were evil and had tested and found some who claimed to be apostles but were indeed imposters. They had not grown weary of being faithful to

His truth. They were also encouraged by the Lord because of their stance of not tolerating the Nicolaitans (Revelation 2:6).

It is key to recognize what the early Church fathers and history said of the Nicolaitans, as it is greatly likened to what we see in culture in this time. They taught that some degree of participation in idolatrous practices of culture was permissible in the Church. They were known as lovers of pleasure, ones given to denigrating speeches and corrupters of their own flesh. They lived lives of unrestrained self-indulgence, sexual perversion, and history speaks of them eating things sacrificed to idols. The temptations and even pressures to become involved with these practices and lifestyle were great since the city's life was dominated by pagan temples.

Ephesus was known as the "temple warden" of the moon goddess Artemis, their adaptation of the Queen of Heaven. Thousands of priests and priestesses served in the temple precincts (Acts 19:35). The city's prosperous economy was partly dependent on trade associated with that temple (Acts 19:23-41). The city had also been declared a "temple warden" of two temples dedicated to the imperial cult, signifying this cult's influence in the city's life. Therefore, the church's resistance to internal pressures to accommodate aspects of this idolatrous society was commendable. This too provides a clarion call for us in our time to do the same. To resist internal and external pressures to accommodate, tolerate, approve, or engage in any form of an idolatrous society. We are to be in this world not of this world.

But then we read of the challenge and course correction issued by the Lord:

But I have this against you, that you have left your first love. Therefore remember from where you have fallen, and repent and do the deeds you did at first; or else I am coming to you and will remove your lampstand out of its place—unless you repent (Revelation 2:4-5 NASB).

The charge for the church of Ephesus, which also applies to each of us, is to remain in a depth of intimacy with Him as our first love. He is to remain as the One who is first, foremost, and in the place of utmost abandoned love in our hearts and lives. We are to welcome Holy Spirit to be the consuming fire in our lives, and He is to remain our heart's desire. We are to continue to burn as His light to this dark world. Therefore, the depth of love that we first had for Him must be guarded, tended, and kept alive. When we feel this love begin to wane, we choose to turn our focus to worship Him, read the Word, welcome Him to come, and fan the flame of passion. To remain in that abiding place, being vitally united to Him. This is not to be a momentary stance but a lifetime consecration, constant, devotion, and honor. What is the resulting inherited promise?

He who has an ear, let him hear what the Spirit says to the churches. To him who overcomes, I will grant to eat of the tree of life which is in the Paradise of God (Revelation 2:7 NASB).

Let's Pray

Father, thank You for the privilege to live during this strategic time in history. I ask that You cause me to continue to be obedient to all You have called me to. May I continue steadfastly in all the deeds You have destined for me. Cause me to walk and live in patient endurance. Holy Spirit, I say that with Your guiding presence and anointing I will not grow weary of being faithful to Your truth and Word. Increase my discernment to know those who are true apostles and those who are not. Cause my discernment to increase to know and walk in Your truth and to be sensitive to not entertain or participate in any sins of practicing idolatry or sexual immorality. Lord, show me any place where I or my family bloodline have tolerated and permitted ungodly beliefs and sinful actions with any form of Queen of Heaven idolatry, sexual immorality, and rituals. And where I (we) have done this, Lord, I ask that You forgive me and my family. And I renounce and evict all demonic assignments and strongholds in my life and the bloodline of my family as a result of Queen of Heaven worship. Lord, where I have walked away from my first love and the passion of love for You, Your presence, Your truth, Your Word, I ask that You forgive me. Holy Spirit, I welcome You to ignite my passion and love for You, Jesus, and my Heavenly Father. Fan into flame the fire and passion again. Be a consuming fire in my life. Anoint me to be the overcomer You have called me to be so at that divinely appointed time I will be granted to eat of the tree of life which is in the Paradise of God. In Jesus' name, amen.

CHURCH OF SMYRNA

I know your tribulation and your poverty (but you are rich), and the blasphemy by those who say they are Jews and are not, but are a synagogue of Satan. Do not fear what you are about to suffer. Behold, the devil is about to cast some of you into prison, so that you will be tested, and you will have tribulation for ten days (Revelation 2:9-10 NASB).

Smyrna was known as the faithful devotee to Rome and all its spiritual and cultural beliefs. It was steeped in the imperial cult worship and also housed temples to Cybele and Zeus. Cybele was the patron goddess of the city, also one of the most ancient forms of Queen of Heaven worship in which her priests were castrated and became eunuchs. It is interesting that this worship was highly revered in Rome during the time of Constantine and many of her pagan ideologies were syncretized into the worship of the Roman Catholic Church among the early followers. Friends, it is vital that within the church, no matter what denomination or affiliation, we ensure that traditions engaged in are not rooted in syncretism with pagan and worldly spiritual practices and ancient principalities. There was great persecution of Christians that occurred in Smyrna while under Roman rule because these believers refused to make sacrifices and bow to the Roman gods. I believe we all see in culture and society that there is an intensified suffering, distress, pressure, and diversity attacking areas such as the spiritual, mental, physical, sexual identity, and finances and economies.

Our Lord states clearly in this passage to not fear. The Greek word for *fear* is *phobeo*. It means "to be frightened, afraid, terrified" (Strong's #G5399). Fear paralyzes faith. Obviously, we live in an era in which there is increasing stress and persecution against Christian faith. We see disturbing turmoil and culture as a whole pulling away from biblical values and principles. Sadly, the more we take God, His love, and His Kingdom principles out of culture, the more anxious and hopeless mankind becomes. Truthfully, these are the goals, objectives, and schemes of these demonic principalities as it was in Smyrna—to paralyze faith, to silence and hinder the message of Jesus, and to thwart the revival, awakening, and transformation He desires to bring and has ordained to transpire.

He is the only true source of joy, peace, and comfort. No amount of human ingenuity or creativity can fill the void left when God is absent. The more He is removed and principalities are given place in a culture and society, fear, anxiety, and worry establish a demonic hold. Our English word *worry* comes from an Anglo-Saxon word that means "to strangle."[2] I think we can all agree that worry certainly does strangle people physically, emotionally, spiritually, and financially. The Bible term *merimnao*, which is often translated "to be careful" or "to be anxious," means literally "to be torn apart."[3]

To be faithful signifies trustworthiness and pertains to a belief that trusts. And He tells us to be faithful even unto death. There are millions of believers today who are suffering and demonically martyred for their Christian walk and faith. While we know there can be a physical death of martyrdom, I fully believe this can also signify our dying daily to Him. That we surrender to Him daily knowing it is Christ, the hope of glory, who is alive in us (Colossians 1:27). And we choose to make Him the center of all that He might live in and through us. And the result is a beautiful Kingdom of Heaven inherited promise:

> *Be faithful until death, and I will give you the crown of life. He who has an ear, let him hear what the Spirit says to the churches. He who overcomes will not be hurt by the second death* (Revelation 2:10-11 NASB).

Let's Pray

Holy Spirit, cause me to be strong in faith during times of trial. Cause me to stand on the truth that where I am weak You are strong. Every place where circumstances, the enemy, or culture attempts to dictate to me that I am poor, I renounce all lies and beliefs that this is my portion and inheritance. Father, Jesus, Holy Spirit, I am rich in and through You. Thank You for this beautiful Kingdom of Heaven promise and inheritance. Cause me not to be influenced by the blasphemy and lies of satan and his army of darkness entrenched within culture. I renounce all blasphemies and lies and their attempt to affect my mind, thoughts, will, and emotions. Lord, deliver me from all evil and give me Your strength, peace, and boldness to not entertain fear nor to walk in fear. I say I have power, love, and a sound mind. I have the spirit of adoption by which I cry out

Abba Father. Help me to hold steadfast, strong, and courageous in trials and persecutions. Help me to be one who is faithful no matter what the cost or price even if it means my life and being faithful unto death. Let my yes to You always be yes. Help me to die daily so that I am transformed from glory to glory into Your image. Make me like You. I say my ears are open to hear what You are saying to the churches. Thank You, Lord, that I will not be hurt by the second death. Amen.

CHURCH OF PERGAMUM

I know where you dwell, where Satan's throne is; and you hold fast My name, and did not deny My faith even in the days of Antipas, My witness, My faithful one, who was killed among you, where Satan dwells. But I have a few things against you, because you have there some who hold the teaching of Balaam, who kept teaching Balak to put a stumbling block before the sons of Israel, to eat things sacrificed to idols and to commit acts of immorality. So you also have some who in the same way hold the teaching of the Nicolaitans (Revelation 2:13-15 NASB).

The believers in Pergamum were holding fast to the Lord's name and not denying their faith. But it speaks here again of those who were following the deviant Nicolaitans. The group had gained a foothold, and, like Balaam of old, the people were encouraged to practice idolatry and sexual immorality

(Numbers 25:1-3; 31:16). It is interesting to note the Balaam was a diviner, soothsayer, seer, and prophet of Mesopotamia—the land and people where Ishtar ruled as Queen of Heaven. Therefore, he was a prophet of Ishtar called on by King Balak to curse the Israelites. Of course, we know the story of the Lord speaking to Balaam through his donkey that in turn halted the agenda of King Balak. This should give us great hope in this time that we live in that our Heavenly Father is able and does move sovereignly in the midst of demonic agendas of great evil and harm.

It is also good to reference the example of Antipas. Why? It explicitly shows the battle of the Queen of Heaven to destroy and kill the Christian faith. History states that in his refusal to deny his faith and to make a sacrifice to the gods, he was taken into the temple of Diana, the Queen of Heaven, placed inside a bronze bull-like altar, and burned alive.

The Lord speaks out a clarion call:

> *Therefore repent [change your inner self—your old way of thinking, your sinful behavior—seek God's will]; or else I am coming to you quickly, and I will make war and fight against them with the sword of My mouth [in judgment]* (Revelation 2:16 AMP).

We, too, must welcome and enter into a deep repenting, purifying work in our lives and come out of these beliefs, practices, and influence of these demonic principalities. The resulting Kingdom of Heaven inherited promise:

He who has an ear, let him hear and heed what the Spirit says to the churches. To him who overcomes [the world through believing that Jesus is the Son of God], to him I will give [the privilege of eating] some of the hidden manna, and I will give him a white stone with a new name engraved on the stone which no one knows except the one who receives it (Revelation 2:17 AMP).

The hidden manna is referring to the glorious relationship we have with Jesus as our hope of glory, which is in great contrast to eating the meat sacrificed to idols. The manna was hidden and covered in the ark of the covenant and now there is glorious manna within our hearts and lives as His believers. What is the significance of this white stone? The Greek word is *psēphos*. This word means little stone, pebble, dressed stone used in mosaics or board games. Other uses or meanings of the white stone are to vote, voice an opinion, and in the legal sphere releasing a verdict.[4] It denotes a small or smooth rounded rock often used for voting in judicial cases; white signified innocence and black signified guilt. We now operate with the white stone in partnering with Him in the verdict and judgment He is releasing against demonic schemes and agendas.

Let's Pray

Jesus, in the midst of darkness and satan's agendas in the world around me, I say that I will hold fast to You and Your name. I ask for continued strength and courage to stand for truth, righteousness, and Your Kingdom even when faithful ones are being persecuted and martyred by demonic, evil agendas. I pray now for all those in the world who are suffering great persecution. Father, give them Your presence, peace, strength, and courage. Bring their cities, regions, and nations freedom to worship You. Holy Spirit, show me every area in my life, my family, my ministry, my business, and within all spheres You have called me into where Balaam's teachings have been allowed to exert an evil, demonic influence and are willingly being held on to. I humbly repent of the activity in my life of being a lover of pleasure, one given to denigrating speeches and corrupters of my flesh. I repent where there has been unrestrained self-indulgence, sexual perversion, and the eating of things and foods sacrificed to idols. Lord, I choose to be the overcomer You have called and positioned me to be. Thank You, Jesus, for hidden manna and entrusting and giving to me a white stone. I choose to use the authority of this white stone and stand in full agreement of Your judgment of satan, the Queen of Heaven, dark principalities, and demons. Thank You for the new name and Kingdom of Heaven identity that I am now walking in. I give You all the honor, glory, and praise. Amen.

CHURCH OF THYATIRA

I know your deeds, and your love and faith and service and perseverance, and that your deeds of late are greater than at first. But I have this against you, that you tolerate the woman Jezebel, who calls herself a prophetess, and she teaches and leads My bond-servants astray so that they commit acts of immorality and eat things sacrificed to idols. I gave her time to repent, and she does not want to repent of her immorality. Behold, I will throw her on a bed of sickness, and those who commit adultery with her into great tribulation, unless they repent of her deeds. And I will kill her children with pestilence, and all the churches will know that I am He who searches the minds and hearts; and I will give to each one of you according to your deeds (Revelation 2:19-23 NASB).

We read that the church of Thyatira was commended for their deeds, love, faith, service, patient endurance. That their last deeds are more numerous and greater than their first. This is a great initial report. However, things quickly change as the Lord addresses their tolerance of Jezebel. The Greek word for *tolerate* is *apheimi,* which means "to permit, give consent to, especially used of a superior to an inferior" (Strong's #G863). We will dedicate an entire chapter to the principality Jezebel. Therefore, I will not go into a deep dive of teaching about her here. However, I will state a few of her demonic manifestations and evil plots. In the natural she was a daughter of King Ethbaal of Sidon, who was a priest in the temple of Astarte, another name and manifestation of Ishtar. Therefore, it is easy to see and recognize that she herself is the embodiment of everything Ishtar represents. A manifestation of seduction, corruption, evil, sexual immorality, idolatry, divination, standing against the prophets of the God, robbing the inheritance from Naboth's vineyard in Jezreel. It is interesting that Issachar was conceived in Jezreel. In reality, her robbing of Naboth's vineyard stands as a direct affront to the prophetic knowing and understanding of times and seasons represented through the sons of Issachar.

It is intriguing to read that Jesus gave her time to repent. This leads to the conclusion that this admonition is not left only to dealing with a principality, but to individuals or leaders who choose to align with this principality, allowing its influence to work in and through them—and who remain completely unrepentant, bringing great demonic deception and harm to the people who follow her. Therefore, it is imperative that we ensure nothing in our lives is tolerating and permitting Jezebel.

To those who do not adhere to or align with Jezebel the following is the promised Kingdom inheritance:

> *But I say to you, the rest who are in Thyatira, who do not hold this teaching, who have not known the deep things of Satan, as they call them—I place no other burden on you. Nevertheless what you have, hold fast until I come. He who overcomes, and he who keeps My deeds until the end, to him I will give authority over the nations; and he shall rule them with a rod of iron, as the vessels of the potter are broken to pieces, as I also have received authority from My Father; and I will give him the morning star. He who has an ear, let him hear what the Spirit says to the churches* (Revelation 2:24-29 NASB).

Great authority is bestowed to those who do not align with Jezebel. It is the authority and power over nations, just as Jesus has been given authority and power over nations by our Heavenly Father.

Let's Pray

Father, thank You for Your faithfulness in my life. I ask that You continue to sustain and strengthen me in love, faith, service, and perseverance in all You have called me to. I humbly come to You and ask You to show me anywhere I or my family bloodline have tolerated, permitted, and aligned with a Jezebel spirit. I repent on behalf of myself and my family bloodline where I (we) have walked in the worship of demon gods and goddesses, sexual immorality, idolatry, shunning and silencing the prophetic, control and manipulation, deception, lying, robbing of inheritance, not sowing financially into Your Kingdom but into the kingdom of darkness. I repent for anywhere in my family bloodline where there was involvement in killing or taking the lives of others. I repent for where I or my family bloodline have not walked in step and in time with You and Your Kingdom and for intentionally delaying and working against Your timing in my life and the lives of others. Thank You, Jesus, for Your forgiveness of sins and cleansing work. In agreement with You I renounce all activity in my life and my family bloodline with a Jezebel spirit. I evict you out of my life and my family bloodline and command you to go now. Holy Spirit, I welcome You to come and fill every place in my spiritual house that has been swept clean and fill me now to overflowing with Your love, peace, truth, joy, life, healing. Cause my spiritual hearing to be opened and pure. I welcome You to speak to me. I want to hear Your voice. Jesus, thank You for the authority to rule with You over nations. Cause me to hear, see, and receive strategies from heaven for revival, a harvest, awakening, and transformation. I give You all the honor, all the glory, and all the praise. In Your name I pray. Amen.

Church of Sardis

He who has the seven Spirits of God and the seven stars, says this: "I know your deeds, that you have a name that you are alive, but you are dead. Wake up, and strengthen the things that remain, which were about to die; for I have not found your deeds completed in the sight of My God" (Revelation 3:1-2 NASB).

Sardis was known as the city of the living dead. It housed one of the largest temples to Artemis in all ancient Greece where sacrifices were made to this demonic entity. Zeus was also worshipped along with the emperor in a portion of the temple. The situation at Sardis requires the exhortation that Jesus gives. The people in this church must come out of their spiritual slumber and sin and wake up and kindle again the burning flame. The reason for His exhortation is that their deeds, both in quality and quantity, are not sufficient to meet the calling to be an awakened and on-fire church impacting a pagan and dark culture. Jesus states what is required to rekindle the flame—remember and repent.

I believe we see in our culture how the influence of demons and principalities has been able to lull many into a place of slumber. As will be shared as we advance in this book, we are called to be the ones who are awake in our spiritual walk, influence, and authority to see His Kingdom come and will be done on earth as it is in heaven.

He then releases His promise for those who hear and overcome:

> *But you have a few people in Sardis who have not soiled their garments; and they will walk with Me in white, for they are worthy. He who overcomes will thus be clothed in white garments; and I will not erase his name from the book of life, and I will confess his name before My Father and before His angels. He who has an ear, let him hear what the Spirit says to the churches* (Revelation 3:4-6 NASB).

Let's Pray

Father, I humbly come before You and repent for all the places in my life where I feel I am alive, but in reality I am spiritually asleep. Forgive me for all places where I have been lulled into slumber and put to sleep. I renounce and evict the spirit of slumber. I say go now in Jesus' name. I proclaim in agreement with You that

I wake up and I am spiritually awake in all areas of my life! Holy Spirit, I welcome You to turn up the heat, to speak clearly when I am entering into partnership with a spirit of slumber. Jesus, I worship and glorify You. I speak that the passion and fire in my life be stirred up and ignited again. Father, I speak that I will walk in purity and the Kingdom authority on the secure foundation of salvation and my Kingdom inheritance as Your ambassador, son/daughter, and friend. I love You, Lord. Amen.

CHURCH OF PHILADELPHIA

He who is holy, who is true, who has the key of David, who opens and no one will shut, and who shuts and no one opens, says this:

"I know your deeds. Behold, I have put before you an open door which no one can shut, because you have a little power, and have kept My word, and have not denied My name. Behold, I will cause those of the synagogue of Satan, who say that they are Jews and are not, but lie—I will make them come and bow down at your feet, and make them know that I have loved you. Because you have kept the word of My perseverance, I also will keep you from the hour of testing, that hour which is about to come upon the whole world, to test those who dwell on the earth. I am coming quickly; hold fast what you have, so that no one will take your crown. He who overcomes, I will make him a pillar in the temple of My God, and

he will not go out from it anymore; and I will write on him the name of My God, and the name of the city of My God, the new Jerusalem, which comes down out of heaven from My God, and My new name. He who has an ear, let him hear what the Spirit says to the churches" (Revelation 3:7-13 NASB).

Philadelphia means "love of the brethren." Brotherly love is an important mark of faith in Jesus. We are taught to love one another and to love our Heavenly Father, Jesus, and Holy Spirit. We must also love a lost world and seek to reach unbelievers with the message of Jesus and to be ones to see His Kingdom established on earth. He has presented us, His Church, His Ekklesia, with this open door.

> Philadelphia was situated in a strategic place on the main route of the Imperial Post from Rome to the East and was called "the gateway to the East." It was also called "little Athens" because of the many pagan temples and hundreds of false gods and goddesses worshipped in the city. This body of believers was certainly positioned in a location of tremendous opportunity.[5]

I believe this is how we must view the time we have been given to live on the earth. We have been divinely positioned and located for tremendous kingdom opportunity, harvest, awakening, and transformation. Jesus has the authority to open and close doors, and these believers were not allowing the darkness of cultural demon gods and goddesses to sway their stance as believers in Jesus and their designation as the Ekklesia of the King of kings and Lord of lords. They knew and stayed steadfast and true to their Kingdom inheritance. They were holding the line!

Isaiah 22:15-25, specifically Isaiah 22:22, is also what is spoken of concerning the keys to the house of David. *"Then I will set on His shoulder the key of the house of David; when he opens no one will shut, when he shuts no one will open"* (AMP). Assyria had invaded Judah (as Isaiah had warned), but the Jewish leaders were trusting Egypt, not our Heavenly Father, to deliver the nation. One of the treacherous leaders was a man named Shebna who used his office, not for the good of the people, but for his own private gain—much like we see in our culture today. The Lord saw to it that Shebna was removed from office and that a faithful man, Eliakim, was put in his place and given the keys of authority. Eliakim was a picture of Jesus and how we as the Church are to operate. In Jewish culture, to carry keys to a house did not suggest someone serving the owner of the house. It signified that full authority was being entrusted as if the one receiving the keys was the master of the house himself. Keys represent Kingdom authority. Just like Eliakim, we too have been bestowed as ones who are dependable administrators of the affairs of the Lord's people and ones who walk in righteous leadership.

An "open door" speaks of Kingdom favor, supernatural, and spiritual authority and a divine opportunity or moment. Just as He gave the church at Philadelphia open doors of great opportunities and *kairos,* meaning strategic moments for Kingdom authority, leadership, and favor, He will do now for each of us.

There were obstacles to overcome. The first was their own lack of strength. The Word tells us that this was not a large or a strong church. However, they were faithful. They were true to His Word and unafraid to be disciples and witnesses of His name. It is important to state a word of encouragement. The size or strength of a body of believers or band of prayer warriors does not determine effectiveness of ministry. Faith in the call and the goodness of the Lord is the key empowerment. I appreciate the revelation stated by Warren Wiersbe, "God's commands are God's enablements. If Jesus gave them an open door, then He would see to it that they were able to walk through it!"[6]

Another obstacle was the opposition of those claiming false identity of being Jews. This group was likened to satan himself in their opposition. Remember, we do not battle against flesh and blood (Ephesians 6:12). Those causing extreme opposition were excluding Jewish believers from the synagogue and also speaking out intense false accusations. Satan is the accuser, and he will use religious people to assist him in speaking out allegations. It is challenging to make Kingdom impact when the leading people in the community are spreading slanderous lies. The church at Smyrna dealt with this manifestation of opposition. The truth is, unbelief sees the difficulties, but faith sees the divine opportunities. Friends, the Lord holds the keys, He has won the victory, no man or woman can close the doors that He has opened. Fear, unbelief, and delay have caused the Church to miss many God-given and divinely orchestrated opportunities.

Three awesome and encouraging promises were given. First, He would take care of their enemies. As we are obedient in the work of His Kingdom, He is faithful to empower us to appropriate victory in battles. One of my favorite quotes from Doris

Wagner is, "The safest place to be is in the center of God's will." And she is so right.

Second, He would keep them from the time of proving and testing. The immediate reference at this point in history would be Roman persecutions, but I also believe that the ultimate reference is to the testing that will involve those on earth who have aligned with satan and his evil agendas before Jesus' return to establish His Kingdom.

The third promise is that He would honor them as pillars. Ancient civilizations often honored great leaders by erecting pillars with their names inscribed on them. Our Heavenly Father's pillars are not made of stone, but I believe those who are His faithful sons and daughters exalt His name for His glory. *"In fact, James, Peter, and John, who were known as pillars of the church, recognized the gift God had given me, and they accepted Barnabas and me as their co-workers"* (Galatians 2:9 NLT).

Friends, we, the Church today, are like the Philadelphia church. He has positioned many with great open doors of opportunity in all realms of society. When He opens the doors, we must walk through. When He shuts doors, we must wait. Above all, we must be faithful to Him and see and seize the opportunities and not be paralyzed or overcome by the obstacles and dark schemes of satan.

Let's Pray

Jesus, I rejoice in You and glorify and worship You as the True and Holy One. You are all truth. You hold the keys of David. What You open no man can shut, and what You shut no man can open. Jesus, cause me to continue to hold true and steadfast to You and Your Kingdom. Thank You for the remnant Church that is on fire for You and walking with You in power and authority. Cause us to increase in this time. That we will arise in spiritual authority to see Shebnas removed and to see Eliakims positioned for such a time as this. Jesus, empower me to be the Kingdom of Heaven influencer and prophetic prayer warrior You have called me to be. To walk in faith that where You have ordained and commanded for me to walk You have also bestowed the full enablement to accomplish what has been assigned. Father, I thank You for the privilege to be a pillar in Your temple and that I am Your son/daughter and will be with You in Your city the new Jerusalem. Amen.

CHURCH OF LAODICEA

To the angel of the church in Laodicea write: The Amen, the faithful and true Witness, the Beginning of the creation of God, says this:

"I know your deeds, that you are neither cold nor hot; I wish that you were cold or hot. So because you are luke-warm, and neither hot nor cold, I will spit you out of My mouth. Because you say, 'I am rich, and have become wealthy, and have need of nothing,' and you do not know that you are wretched and miserable and poor and blind and naked, I advise you to buy from Me gold refined by

fire so that you may become rich, and white garments so that you may clothe yourself, and that the shame of your nakedness will not be revealed; and eye salve to anoint your eyes so that you may see. Those whom I love, I reprove and discipline; therefore be zealous and repent. Behold, I stand at the door and knock; if anyone hears My voice and opens the door, I will come in to him and will dine with him, and he with Me. He who overcomes, I will grant to him to sit down with Me on My throne, as I also overcame and sat down with My Father on His throne. He who has an ear, let him hear what the Spirit says to the churches" (Revelation 3:14-22 NASB).

Laodicea was very wealthy. In fact, in my studies, I discovered that they manufactured a special eye salve. In His address to the Church, He made the declaration that He is "the Amen." The Hebrew word for *amen* is defined "surely it is true" (Strong's #H589). In this encounter, He is now speaking the truth to their spiritually blind condition. It was a hard truth, but what was needed to give the invitation to enter in and be passionately ignited once more for Him. Let's look at the four areas highlighted for the church to overcome.

They Lost the Fire of a Burning Heart

The three spiritual temperatures He emphasized were a burning heart, a cold heart, which often becomes a hard heart, and the lukewarm heart. Those who are lukewarm are comfortable, complacent, and indifferent. Sadly, those who have reached this state are often unaware of their condition. As believers in Jesus, we must be fervent in our spiritual lives and fervent in our intercessory pursuit of Him.

Jesus said, *"Without Me you can do nothing"* (John 15:5 NKJV). Friends, the Laodicean church had grown independent, self-satisfied, and secure in their own wealth and, therefore, in need of nothing. But all the while, their spiritual power had been diminishing and dying. Their material wealth and glowing accomplishments were masking their spiritual decline. Jesus was outside the church, trying to get in.

They Lost Their Values

It's interesting that the church in Smyrna thought they were poor when our Father's evaluation was they were rich. The Laodicean church boasted that they were rich, but His assessment called them poor. Maybe this gives us a hint of another reason for their spiritual decline. There absolutely is the righteous call for Kingdom wealth for Kingdom blessings and purposes. However, they seemed to have become proud and measured their value more on material gain than spiritual values and gain. The Lord did not mince His words—in His eyes they were wretched, miserable, poor, blind, and naked (Revelation 3:17).

As previously stated, Laodicea was a wealthy city with their banking center housed inside the temple. Therefore, their wealth was sacred to the demon gods and goddesses. No one would dare rob or touch sacred finances. Perhaps some of the corrupt spirit of the time in the marketplace had crept its way into the church and it negatively influenced them, twisting their values. Whereas the Church was to be His righteous standard bearers of Kingdom of Heaven wealth.

What was His expressed solution? Pay the price to get the true gold that is refined in the fire. The Greek word *pyr* means "fire, combustion of material, bonfire, a relatively large camp-fire for warming a group, that which causes discord, and a place of punishment such as hell" (Strong's #G4442). In essence, He is clearly communicating about the revival and awakening we all must allow in our lives—His consuming and refining fire to cleanse every and all impurities. Stirring our hearts to walk in a deep place of abiding intimacy where the fire on the altar is kindled and it does not go out.

They Had Lost Their Sight

They were blind and unable to see their true reality. The apostle Peter teaches that when a believer is not growing in the Lord, his spiritual vision is affected (2 Peter 1:5-9). The Laodiceans could not see themselves as they really were. Nor could they see the Lord as He stood outside the door of the church, knocking. They were unable to see the spiritual open doors of opportunity right before them. They were so focused on building their own agenda that they had become lukewarm in their pursuit of Him and their call to impact the dark world.

The solution? They were in great need of His spiritual healing eye salve in place of their manufactured healing salve. The eye is one of the body's most sensitive areas. The work of Holy Spirit is so necessary to operate on and touch our spiritual sight to cause it to be opened. We must submit to Him, welcome Him to open our spiritual eyes, and then maintain and walk in the abiding place with Him so we see and discern what He wants us to see.

They Had Lost Their Spiritual Garments

To be naked meant to be defeated and humiliated. The Laodiceans could go to the market and purchase fine woolen garments, but that would not meet their real need. They needed the white garments of Jesus' righteousness and grace. Salvation means that Jesus' righteousness is accredited to us, put to our account. Sanctification means that His righteousness is imparted to us to awaken us to our identity in Him, therefore impacting our character to transform us from glory to glory into His image.

There is no praise given to this assembly. They thought they were glorifying our Heavenly Father, Jesus, and Holy Spirit. But the sad reality was that they were disgracing His name just as though they had been walking around naked. In response the Lord issued three directives.

First, He spoke of His love and discipline, "*Those whom I love, I reprove and discipline*" (Revelation 3:19 NASB). He still loved them, even though their love for Him had grown cold.

Second, He gave an exhortation, "*Be zealous and repent*" (Revelation 3:19 NASB). The church at Laodicea had to repent of their pride and humble themselves before the Lord. They had to stir up that inner fire and cultivate a burning heart.

Third, He extended an invitation, "*Behold, I stand at the door and knock; if anyone hears My voice and opens the door, I will come in to him and will dine with him, and he with Me*" (Revelation 3:20-22 NASB). Here He begins to speak to the heart of the individual, "*if anyone*" (Revelation 3:20 NASB), and not to the whole congregation. He appealed to a small remnant in Sardis, and now He appeals to the individual. He can do great things through one surrendered, dedicated man or woman.

Friends, our Heavenly Father is so good. Jesus is so, so good. He was not and is not impatient. He stood at the doors of the hearts of the people and stands at the doors of our hearts. He knocks. He wants to come in, to have fellowship, to commune, and to have an intimate relationship with the ones who will hear, respond, and be awakened to a surrendered abiding in Him. When we invite Him in, the banquet table becomes a throne room. It is through relationship with Him that we find victory and become the overcomers He has destined us to be.

Let's Pray

Jesus, I glorify and worship You as the Amen and the Truth. Thank You that in knowing You and knowing Your truth that I am set free. I humbly come before You and repent in all areas where I am neither hot nor cold, but lukewarm. I repent where I have lost the burning and fire of a fervent heart. Lord, I repent where I have lost Kingdom values and put more trust in man-made wealth. I repent for every instance when, knowingly or unknowingly, I laid my finances at the feet of demons, demonic agendas, and cultural demonic altars. I repent for trusting in my own strength, the ways of man, and the world and building my own kingdom. I repent for being naked and blind and all areas where I have lost spiritual sight and vision. I repent for not hearing You when You have stood at the door of my heart and life and I have not opened the door. Thank You for Your forgiveness. I now open my heart and say yes to You and welcome more of You in my life. Jesus, I say yes to sitting at Your table and dining and feasting with You. Cause me to walk as the victorious overcomer You have positioned me to be. Father, I rejoice, say yes, and stand in the authority and position You have bestowed on me as Your child. I am seated with You in heavenly places. You have bestowed authority to trample on serpents and scorpions and all the power of the enemy. You are the victorious King of All and I glorify You this day and forevermore. In Your name I pray, amen!

Moving Onward

Now that we have discovered and walked through a cleansing and awakening journey, let's advance into learning and awakening the authority He bestows to us, His Church.

Chapter Three

CALLED AND CHOSEN TO CONQUER

They will wage war against the Lamb (Christ), and the Lamb will triumph and conquer them, because He is Lord of lords and King of kings, and those who are with Him and on His side are the called and chosen (elect) and faithful (Revelation 17:14 AMP).

In this taken-up encounter, John is shown and told, "The Lord will conquer them." This is referring to the Queen of Heaven, Babylon, worldwide power, the beast that she rides on, the seven heads and ten horns who make up this demonic kingdom and who partnered together in fulfilling their global evil satanic schemes. Many scholars say that the seven heads are seven mountains (high places, possibly the seven hills of Rome). Also, they could be seven kings or seven kingdoms. While I do not consider myself a theologian on releasing a full explanation concerning the seven heads and ten horns, I find it interesting that heads can also denote a point of time at the very start of a duration, a new era.[1] The ten horns, as is depicted, represent ten kings or powers who have not received a kingdom and who unite to give their authority over to the beast. The redemptive and victorious news is the Lord and all who are with Him will conquer this demonic army. The Greek word for *conquer* is *nikao* meaning "to win a victory over, to be victorious over, to be a victor, to conquer" (Strong's #G3528).

This scripture also shares that we are called and chosen. The word for *called* is *miq·rā* signifying an assembly, group, convocation, a collective of people gathered for a purpose (Strong's #G2282). The Greek word for *chosen* is *ekletos* denoting someone whose participation or presence has been officially requested (for something); carrying the sense that is a request to which refusal is not an option, as in being summoned and commissioned as an apostle.[2] In further studies, the chosen ones are faithful ones singled out from others to some honorable service or station. "These chosen warriors are a class that are picked out as the most valiant and skillful in an army, best adapted to some special and momentous enterprise."[3]

In the culmination of the finality and victorious moment when the Lord deals the ultimate end to Babylon, we read that there will be a great confusion in satan's schemes and in his ranks, which has been the divine and ordained plan of the Lord all along. I believe the Lord sometimes will allow satan to believe he has won, and suddenly His victorious, conquering plan is majestically made known. The beast, seven heads, and ten kings will turn on the Queen of Heaven, this satanic structure of Babylon will be destroyed by fire, and her Babylonian kingdom that has influenced people, multitudes, nations, and languages will fall (Revelation 17:15 and Revelation 18).

AUTHORITY OF THE CHOSEN

That being said, as we continue the discussion of our warfare mandate and stance in dealing with the principality of Babylon, it is vital that we understand as His chosen warriors we are appropriating the victory and triumph over satan and his evil, dark army that was secured by Jesus' death on the cross, resurrection from the grave, and ascension to the throne at the right hand of our Father.

Jesus disarmed principalities and made a public spectacle of them.

Having disarmed principalities and powers, He made a public spectacle of them, triumphing over them in it (Colossians 2:15 NKJV).

Jesus is exalted first above every ruler.

And [so that you will begin to know] what the immeasurable and unlimited and surpassing greatness of His [active, spiritual] power is in us who believe. These are in accordance with the working of His mighty strength which He produced in Christ when He raised Him from the dead and seated Him at His own right hand in the heavenly places, far above all rule and authority and power and dominion [whether angelic or human], and [far above] every name that is named [above every title that can be conferred], not only in this age and world but also in the one to come (Ephesians 1:19-21 AMP).

All things are under Jesus' feet.

And He put all things [in every realm] in subjection under Christ's feet (Ephesians 1:22 AMP).

Jesus is the Head of the Church.

And appointed Him as [supreme and authoritative] head over all things in the church, which is His body, the fullness of Him who fills and completes all things in all [believers] (Ephesians 1:22-23 AMP).

Jesus Himself tells of His authority.

Jesus approached and, breaking the silence, said to them, All authority (all power of rule) in heaven and on earth has been given to Me (Matthew 28:18 AMPC).

The above are just a few of the scriptures we can quote speaking of the authority of our Risen King. As quoted, He is the Head of the Church. He is all authority. And He, as the head, bestows to us *"the authority to trample on serpents and scorpions, and over all the power of the enemy"* (Luke 10:19 NKJV). And as Paul expresses to the Ephesians as one of his burning desires *"that through the church the complicated, many-sided wisdom of God in all its infinite variety and innumerable aspects might now be made known to the angelic rulers and authorities (principalities and powers) in the heavenly sphere"* (Ephesians 3:10 AMPC).

Here is a clear directive from the Head to us the Body, His called, chosen, and faithful warriors. The scribed word from

Paul explicitly states that the Church should make this declaration to the rulers and authorities in the heavenly places. There are many interpretations as to what this might mean, but one of them would be that we are to declare the gospel of the Kingdom of God. These rulers and authorities are the same demonic forces Paul speaks of in Ephesians 6:12, *"Our battle is with the highest principalities and authorities operating in rebellion under heavenly realms"* (TPT). Therefore, the Church, by deed and also by word, is to remind rulers, authorities, and powers such as the Queen of Heaven and her Babylonian structure that the Kingdom of our God has invaded the kingdom of darkness beginning with the life, death, resurrection, and ascension of Jesus. And we are going to take our place in the chosen army of the Lord to see to it that the god of this age will no longer blind the minds of unbelievers to the glorious message of Jesus and we will engage in strategies from heaven to defeat rulers and authorities so the breaking forth of revival, awakening, and transformation is made manifest.

PAY HER BACK DOUBLE FOR HER TORMENT

Repay to her even as she has repaid others, and pay back [to her] double [her torment] in accordance with what she has done; in the cup [of sin and suffering] which she mixed, mix a double portion [of perfect justice] for her (Revelation 18:6 AMP).

What a grave and fateful directive. It is beyond evident that the Lord means business and He wants this principality defeated and His already ordained judgment of complete conquering and destruction by fire realized. After calling us, His people, to come out from her, He then begins to declare how the defeat and conquering of this demonic Babylonia Queen of Heaven structure will victoriously and triumphantly unfold.

The Greek word used for *repay* in the above referenced Revelation 18:6 is *apodidōmi*. It means "pay or pay back, with the implication of payment of an incurred obligation." It also is defined as recompense, whether positive or not, and carries with it the sense to reward or punish (whether tangible or intangibly) based upon what a person deserves (Strong's #G591). Pay back to her double stems from the Geek word *diploo* meaning we give her twice the deeds (torment) that she has given (Strong's #G1363). Friends, this is not spoken in a love language, but an all-out conquer and destroy language. I will state this for clarity's sake. While we know private revenge is forbidden and that our battle is not against flesh and blood, our Heavenly Father will have us, His people, act under Him, when called to it, in pulling down His and our deep-rooted, ruthless, relentless, and evil spiritual enemies.

The truth is, there is a rendering that the Lord has ordained and destined for the Queen of Heaven and Babylon. His rendering is that she will be mixed a double portion of perfect justice and a double portion of torment that she has rendered to people and nations in her diabolical schemes and agendas. Why? Our Heavenly Father is not willing that any should perish. Trust me, in my thirty-four years of ministry across our nation and the nations (forty-eight at this point in time) in which extensive historical research and strategic intercession have occurred, it is scripturally revealed and also my firm belief that our Father hates the Queen of Heaven and all demonic principalities. It is astonishing to see all the evil, perversion, wickedness, governmental corruption, persecution, economic corruption, seduction, idolatry, bondage, hopelessness, torment, and death that this satanic principality has unleashed in the nations of the world. The Lord explains in Revelation 17 who she sits enthroned over and who she wields her power against: *"the great harlot who sits on many waters"* (Revelation 17:1 NASB). And what are the waters? *"The waters which you saw, where the harlot sits, are peoples, multitudes, nations, and tongues"* (Revelation 17:15 NKJV). He is unwavering in His judgment being fully rendered to her. The same evil and depraved manner in which she brought demonic justice and torment is to be rendered back to her. Many theologians state that in this action of rendering He is making an appeal, requisition, demand, and summons to those who are conquering this corrupt structure with Him. Who are those He is speaking of in the summoning? Studies that I believe to be true indicate it is Himself, the angels, and His people.

She Glorified Herself as Queen

To the degree that she glorified herself and reveled and gloated in her sensuality [living deliciously and luxuriously], to that same degree impose on her torment and anguish, and mourning and grief; for in her heart she boasts, "I sit as a queen [on a throne] and I am not a widow, and will never, ever see mourning or experience grief" (Revelation 18:7 AMP).

The demonic veil is lifted and full exposure of the outright arrogant, self-proclaiming evil of this demonic system is revealed. Her three proclaimed statements give clear evidence to this fact.

- I sit as queen as the mistress of the world, the finest city of all time.
- I am not a widow because all the world's kings are my lovers.
- I will never mourn for I am emphatically in control of my destiny.

The evil intent along with motives were also shown to Isaiah and exposed in the prophetic word he released in Isaiah 47:7-9 (NLT):

> You said, "I will reign forever as queen of the world!" You did not reflect on your actions or think about their consequences. Listen to this, you pleasure-loving kingdom, living at ease and feeling secure. You say, "I am the only one, and there is no other. I will never be a widow or lose my children." Well, both these things will come upon you in a moment: widowhood and the loss of your children. Yes, these calamities will come upon you, despite all your witchcraft and magic.

It is important to be aware that the Lord is very specific in His punishment to the enemy and his demonic army. He is exact and precise in His punishment for how satan and his demons have interrupted relationship between Himself and humankind. Hell was never meant for God's children, so as a protective Father He exacts His vengeance in a specific way to this evil spiritual army of darkness. What do I mean by this? Every area where this Queen of Heaven and all other demonic entities have attempted to rule supreme the Lord exacts His rendering blow of judgment. I want to remind you again that we are speaking of dealing with a demonic principality in the spiritual realm. As this is done, her wicked ways controlling wealth and kingdoms will be defeated and Kingdom of Heaven harvest, wealth, and transformation realized.

She claims she will reign forever, meaning an eternity as queen. To achieve this, she positioned herself at the entrance gates of kingdoms, altars of temples, and hearts of the people within her kingdoms. All of these were not only dedication sites but gates and altars of time. And through the magic rituals and occult enchantments done in worship of her, her priests and prophets demonically manipulated destinies, culture, and time. Therefore, the Lord is declaring His Kingdom is now set in place in all time and history and her occult grip on time is broken.

She says she is no widow but that is exactly what our Heavenly Father ensures that she is. Kings that she thought were with her turn against her. The wealth of kings, kingdoms, and merchants gained in her honor and to her honor will be laid waste, meaning her evil ways of gaining wealth to hold peoples and nations in bondage will be destroyed. Her acts of sexually perverse rituals to empower kings will end. Therefore, she is now the widow in mourning.

> *For this reason in a single day her plagues (afflictions, calamities) will come, pestilence and mourning and famine* (Revelation 18:8 AMP).

Where she was worshipped to ensure fertility, her demonic womb is now barren. Where she took life, sacrificed children on the altar, exacted killing and murder as the goddess of war she will now experience plagues and an eternity of mourning, anguish, and death. Where she was the one her devotees believed ensured that the harvest was plentiful, she will now be in anguish of deep hunger that is never satisfied.

BURNED IN FIRE

And she will be burned up with fire and completely consumed; for strong and powerful is the Lord God who judges her (Revelation 18:8 AMP).

I believe we have clear prophetic insight. The Lord is serious in His judgment against this foe, her demonic structure and world system. He says that she will be burned in the fire and completely consumed. The Greek word for *fire* in this scripture is *pyr* (Strong's #G4442). One definition of this word is punishment and hell. But I want to take the time here to exhort us, the chosen band of warriors. It is fire that will bring her destruction, so therefore it is essential for us, personally and corporately, to walk in revival and awakening fire as we advance as His victorious, faithful ones. Why? First and foremost, we want to have that abiding place with our Heavenly Father, Jesus, and Holy Spirit. It should be a burning desire in us because we genuinely want to walk in a sold-out, surrendered, intimate relationship with the Lord.

This is so vitally important. I have been involved in intercession for many years. I have walked with many prophetic intercessors and spiritual warriors. And many are weary, have stopped praying, or have lost their passion and fire. Jesus states in Luke 12:49, "*I have come to set the earth on fire. And how I long for every heart to be already ablaze with this fiery passion for God*" (TPT). The word for *fire* in this scripture is also *pyr*, the same word for punishment and hell. In this context, Jesus isn't saying He desires to bring punishment to us. He is emphasizing the other meanings of this word, which is a consuming fire, a bonfire that is set ablaze and causes warmth for us personally and others who come near the fire. He is referring to the fire of passion for Him and His Kingdom that He desires to ignite in each of us. *Ablaze* means "to cause the process of burning to begin, to ignite, to kindle, to set ablaze, to start a fire, to light a lamp." What are we set ablaze with? Passion—a cry for more of Him, a willingness to allow Him to be a consuming fire in our lives. That we, as the temple of the Lord, allow our lives and bodies to be a living sacrifice for Him and that the fire on the altar of our hearts and lives never go out.

In February of 2019, I had a profound encounter. I was in intercession in the night hours. Holy Spirit asked me a question. "Becca, do you really know Me?" I was surprised by what He asked. I have been filled and baptized with Holy Spirit since 1990. I asked Him if He would repeat the question. He inquired again, "Becca, do you really know Me?" I knew in that instant what the meaning was behind His question. He was asking me to search my heart to discover if I had grown comfortable in the level of relationship I had with Him. Was there still a desire to grow deeper in my relationship with Him? Was there still a hunger for more of Him? Had my passion waxed cold? Had I grown weary in well doing, therefore, my relationship with Him was not burning in that same place of passion as it had before? I realized that my answer was, "Yes." I still absolutely loved Him, but I had grown weary in my busy schedule, which in turn caused my passion to be weary. I asked Holy Spirit to forgive me and to fan into flame the passion in my heart for Him once more. He made this statement to me: "In the Church, there has been so much form without My fire."

Friends, I have been so intentional since that time to ensure that my passion for Him and my personal relationship with Him stays in a place of being first and foremost. I have even welcomed Him and made this invitation to Him, "Holy Spirit, any place where my love for You is growing cold or beginning to ebb, turn up the heat of Your presence, conviction, and fire in my life. Holy Spirit, cause my passion and love for You to burn with a holy fire."

Why do I write about this in a chapter discussing that we are called and chosen to conquer with Him in spiritual warfare? Because if this place is not first and foremost in our lives, we will not have the endurance, perseverance, tenacity to advance. For the disciples to do all they did for the Lord, it took a deep relationship, baptism, and presence of Holy Spirit to move in *dunamis* power in order to see lives changed and cities and regions turned upside down for the Kingdom of God. Allow me to expound a bit more.

We are all familiar with Acts 2 and when the Holy Spirit fell at Pentecost.

Suddenly, there was a sound from heaven like the roaring of a mighty windstorm, and it filled the house where they were sitting. Then, what looked like flames or tongues of fire appeared and settled on each of them. And everyone present was filled with the Holy Spirit (Acts 2:2-4 NLT).

When studying the translation of the words *mighty rushing wind*, a clear and descriptive picture of what transpired is established. This wind was mighty and it carried a force, impact, and burden. As it rushed in, it went to the very deepest part of a man or woman that is able to respond to God. They were suddenly, instantly filled with the very breath of life of God Himself, Holy Spirit. And when they were filled, their minds, thoughts, emotions, and belief in spirit-realm encounters were instantaneously transformed into a new paradigm and a Kingdom of God way of thinking. It was a sudden and drastic change that filled each of them with boldness, joy, and fire, with tongues of fire distributed on each of them. The fire *(pyr)* of Holy Spirit anointed and empowered each of them and they were set aflame, a burning torch.

Let's depict this in an even clearer picture. Instead of looking at the burning bush, they became the burning bush. The burning ones commissioned by God Himself to go out and boldly proclaim the gospel, to see a harvest come forth, and to literally carry an empowerment to dramatically turn the world upside down for the Kingdom of God. Holy Spirit is this wind—the very breath of God, the fire carrying the glory and His *ruach*, His breath of life that comes into the deepest part of a man or woman who can respond to Him. Just as the 120 were filled, we too are completely filled, transformed from the inside out, and emboldened with His fire and glory to move and advance His Kingdom in this lost world.

I fully believe the fire of His presence, His breath of life, His purifying, consuming fire, His glory in our lives determines the extent of the effective impact and breakthrough we will incur in spiritual warfare. We must burn on fire for Him and stand on the firm foundation of our relationship with Him to be unwavering in the power and authority He has bestowed in and through us to see principalities defeated and conquered. The greatest lovers make the greatest warriors because we have a cause to fight from and to fight for. We war from heaven to earth, from His presence, glory, and fire. We don't fight for victory but from victory and with victory.

REJOICE APOSTLES AND PROPHETS

What is to be our response when we see this principality defeated and conquered and Babylon fall? I love the declaration that is resounded out. *"Rejoice over her, O heaven, and you saints and apostles and prophets, because God has pronounced judgment for you against her"* (Revelation 18:20 NASB). The Greek word in this scripture for *joy* is *euphrainō.* It means "make glad, cause celebration, have a feeling or attitude of joy and happiness and making an outward expression of that joy" (Strong's #G2370). When we see the Queen of Heaven and her evil schemes defeated we are to celebrate and rejoice.

REJOICING IN THE HEAVENS

What is heaven's response? Revelation 19 is titled (in some translations) the fourfold hallelujah with the loud voice of a great multitude in all-out rejoicing, joy, celebration, and worship to our King.

> *Hallelujah! Salvation and glory and power belong to our God; because His judgments are true and righteous; for He has judged the great harlot who was corrupting the earth with her immorality, and He has avenged the blood of His bond-servants on her* (Revelation 19:1-2 NASB).

> *And a second time they said, "Hallelujah! Her smoke rises up forever and ever"* (Revelation 19:3 NASB).

> *And the twenty-four elders and the four living creatures fell down and worshiped God who sits on the throne saying, "Amen. Hallelujah!" And a voice came from the throne, saying, "Give praise to our God, all you His bond-servants, you who fear Him, the small and the great"* (Revelation 19:4-5 NASB).

> *Then I heard something like the voice of a great multitude and like the sound of many waters and like the sound of mighty peals of thunder, saying, "Hallelujah! For the Lord our God, the Almighty, reigns"* (Revelation 19:6 NASB).

> *"Let us rejoice and be glad and give the glory to Him, for the marriage of the Lamb has come and His bride has made herself ready"* (Revelation 19:7 NASB).

Wow! When the called, chosen, and faithful ones rise to advance, when He summons us to advance with Him and we see His appropriated victory manifested, great celebration and praise among the people and heaven is demonstrated.

WHAT IF?

As we move forward, I would like to pose a question. What if? What if we seek the Lord for the prophetic warfare assignments He is calling us to and carry them out to fullness? What if we all choose to walk in revival, awakening, and transformation? What if we say yes as His chosen spiritual warriors to the assignments He is calling us to in the territories, regions, and spheres of influence to see the Queen of Heaven and her many manifestations plundered and defeated? I believe we are in that strategic moment in history of the greatest awakening and move of His Spirit in the hearts of men, women, and families. A strategic moment in time when we see peoples and regions gripped by principalities, evil, depravity, and darkness set free. Where brothers have turned against brothers, nations turned against nations there will be a coming out from her and defeating, conquering, and unseating of this ancient principality. We will see His Kingdom come, His will be done on earth as it is in heaven.

Chapter Four

ISHTAR

The ancient region of Mesopotamia was home to the first civilizations in human history, or as some also call it the cradle of civilization. From roughly 3200 BC to the fall of the Persian Empire in 331 BC, the Sumerians, Akkadians, Babylonians, and Assyrians made their home between the Tigris and Euphrates River. As a reminder, these cultures worshipped a diverse number of deities that held sway and power over every area of their lives, culture, society, and government. As previously mentioned, one of the most complex and powerful principalities was the goddess Ishtar, the Queen of Heaven, the goddess of love, sex, and war. Below are words from an ancient hymn written in worship to her.

Who is it that could rival her grandeur?
Her attributes are mighty, splendid, superb.
Ishtar this is, who could rival her grandeur?
Her attributes are mighty, splendid, superb.
She it is who stands foremost among the gods,
Her word is the weightiest, it prevails over theirs.
Ishtar stands foremost among the gods,

Her word is the weightiest, it prevails over theirs.
She is their queen, they discuss her commands,
All of them bow down before her:
They go to her (in) her radiance,
Women and man fear her too.[1]

Some of you might be pondering how an ancient principality could still have a demonic grip and hold on society and culture today. After all, she was the ancient goddess of an ancient civilization. We are living in an era thousands of years removed from this demonic principality and its evil agenda and dark demonic grip. How could this possibly have impact on us now? Greg and I discovered professionally etched on a window at Denver International Airport, "From the great above the goddess opened her ear to the great below, from the great above Inanna opened her ear to the great below." This was a convincing and shocking discovery. Friends, this Queen of Heaven is actively entrenched in our culture.

One strategy that is key to remember at this point of discussion, and that will be applied throughout the remainder of this teaching, is we must look to the original root bondage where the principality established its demonic throne over spheres of influence, cities, regions, nations. It is necessary and strategic to look at the original sin that gave this principality power and authority. This is one spiritual warfare principle that has been made evident throughout history and time—satan and his army of darkness hate to lose their hold. Therefore, to be empowered and effective warriors we look to the original bondage of these entities and the captivity they established over people and culture. Then also the resulting prevailing bondage, which is the systematic recurrence through time and history of the original root bondage. This provides great wisdom and spiritual insight in order that we are aware of the wiles of the enemy so that he might not outwit us. Principalities are looking for an open door of sin, altars of worship, bloodshed, covenant breaking, idolatry, and perversion to welcome the next opportunity of empowerment in order to seat themselves and advance in their demonic agendas from generation to generation. In my books *Authority to Tread* and *Glory Warfare*, I give a full understanding of this principle. So let's look at Ishtar throughout history and time and the gates of culture over which she has been seated.

HER ORIGINS

Ishtar's origins can be traced back to the Sumerian goddess Inanna, with whom she shares many attributes and myths. Over time, as cultures merged within the Mesopotamian region, Ishtar became a prominent figure in the pantheons of various Mesopotamian peoples, including the Akkadians, Babylonians, and Assyrians.

Her significance in these societies was profound, dark, and complex, personifying the central characters of femininity and sovereignty, while also representing the terrifying aspects of nature, love and war. It was said that she could soothe and bring venom. That she could create that which was deemed impossible to create and destroy what should not be destroyed. She was the goddess of fire. She could nurture and bring life, but then be aggressive, angry, and kill. She was known as the goddess of gates and one who stood in authority at the gates. She was a seductress and through perversion her worship was perpetuated. She crossed all cultural boundaries, and where she ruled supreme great confusion and chaos would be seen. She explicitly illustrates the Mesopotamians' belief in and acknowledgement of the dual properties of existence, where creation and destruction are entwined.

BELIEFS AND WORSHIP PRACTICES

The worship of Ishtar was widespread with major temples dedicated to her in cities such as Uruk, Babylon, and Nineveh. Worship, rituals, ceremonies, and festivals in her honor played an integral role in the culture and society. To understand the significance of these festivals, we must briefly share the demonic myths or legends surrounding Ishtar.

> Many of her myths involve her [aggressiveness in] taking over the domain of other deities. She was believed to have been given the mes, which represented all positive and negative aspects of civilization, by Enki, the god of wisdom. She was also believed to have taken over the Eanna temple from An, the god of the sky. Alongside her twin brother Utu (later known as Shamash), Inanna [Ishtar] was the enforcer of divine justice; she destroyed Mount Ebih for having challenged her authority.[2]

Two of the most prominent notable myths of Ishtar are the *Epic of Gilgamesh* and the *Descent of Ishtar to the Underworld*. In the *Epic of Gilgamesh*, her romantic advances toward the hero Gilgamesh and his subsequent rejection of Ishtar enrages her.

She calls on the Bull of Heaven to kill Gilgamesh. But instead, the Bull of Heaven is killed by Gilgamesh.

Another legend, *The Descent of Ishtar into the Underworld*, depicts her traveling to the Netherworld to gain dominion over the kingdom of the dead. Her sister, Ereshkigal, is the ruler of this realm. She is angry with Ishtar and requires her to travel through seven gates descending further into the realm of darkness where at every entrance she is to disrobe all vestiges of her queenly authority. As Ishtar finally arrives unclothed in the presence of her sister, Ereshkigal kills her. After three days, Ishtar's faithful companion Ninshubur approaches the god of wisdom Enki to help in rescuing the dead Ishtar. It is interesting to learn that Ninshubur when with Ishtar was a female. When she served other gods she was male. Enki agrees to help and creates two beings who are neither male nor female. In Sumerian texts they were called *galatur*. In Akkadian texts, *kurgarrū* and *assinnu*. They are able to trick Ereshkigal to release Ishtar under the condition that someone takes Ishtar's place.[3]

Dumuzi, known as Tammuz in the Bible (Ezekiel 8:14), is said to be both Ishtar's husband and lover. Before her journey to the underworld, the story of Ishtar's legend reports she and Dumuzi were enthralled in a great love story. However, when Ishtar returns from the dead, she witnesses Dumuzi reveling, joyful, celebrating. He was not sad nor was he missing his dead wife. Ishtar, again, becomes angry and has him sent to the Underworld in her place. From this point, he spends six months of the year held captive in the Underworld and six months of the year in heaven with Ishtar. As we will discover, the festivals celebrating

Ishtar's mythological journey to the underworld and back were significant religious events symbolizing the cycle of death and rebirth and the seasonal renewal of the earth.

I realize all of this sounds like it should be some sort of fantasy movie out of Hollywood. It is amazing and a little mind blowing when we read the beliefs and worship practices behind Ishtar and other demonic principalities and how steeped cultures were in the beliefs and worship of these demonic beings. What gives this principality and story a right to grip cultures? When humankind falls into sin and partners with, empowers, or worships these principalities, they are then welcomed in to begin their evil rule over spheres of influence, cities, cultures, nations. Again, an in-depth teaching on these principles can be found in my books *Authority to Tread* and *Glory Warfare.*

Priests, Priestesses, Rituals, and Festivals

Within Ishtar's temples, priests and priestesses played crucial roles in mediating between the divine and the mortal realms. These religious figures were not only spiritual leaders but also keepers of ancient rites and traditions that facilitated the connection of the populace with the divine.

A special group of male priests, often described in historical texts as transgender or transvestite, served the goddess by performing rituals and ceremonies that often involved cross-dressing and adopting roles traditionally associated with the opposite gender. These individuals, known as *gala* in Sumerian or *kurgarrū* and *assinnu* in Akkadian, are thought to have transcended typical gender roles to embody the goddess's dual nature. She herself was viewed as androgynous, embodying both feminine and masculine characteristics and noted to have witchcraft empowerment to turn a man into a woman or a woman into a man.

Let's briefly discuss the *gala*. These were priests of the Ishtar cult and the Cybele cult. These male priests would worship themselves into an ecstatic demonic frenzy and trance at her altar, and at the point of climax castrate themselves. After their complete dedication to these entities in this beyond disturbing act of worship, they would then become known as eunuchs, dressing themselves as women.

The women priests and temple workers were known as the *harimtu*, the *kezertu*, the *samhatu*, and the *istaru*. They engaged in sacred prostitution outside of marriage, the act being done with men. Therefore, they stood in direct breach of the marriage covenant. Ishtar herself was said to engage in what was termed sacred marriage, *heiros gamos*, sexual activity with the king to ensure her rule and empowerment over culture.[4] This is still practiced in modern culture within Wicca. The call it the Wiccan Great Rite.

High priests often oversaw the temple's operations, including ritual performances, maintenance of sacred spaces, and the management of offerings and sacrifices. Priestesses, sometimes referred to as *hierodules* or sacred prostitutes, also participated in rites that involved sacred sexuality, a practice believed to ensure fertility and prosperity for the community and land. These were also involved in teaching, healing, and divination, serving as intermediaries and prophets who interpreted and communicated the will of Ishtar to the people.

Festivals, particularly the New Year's festival of *Akitu*, celebrated Ishtar's role in renewal and creation, featuring processions, music, and sacred dramas. Sexual rites performed by priestesses were done with the intent to embody the fertility aspect of her worship, believed to bring divine blessings of abundance. Sacrifices and offerings of food, drink, and precious items were also central to worship practices, intended to appease the goddess and ensure her benevolence.

The Significance of Sacred Spaces

Temples dedicated to Ishtar served as central hubs for worship, housing both the divine statue of the goddess and the community of priests and priestesses who served her. These sacred spaces were designed to be a reflection of the heavenly realm on earth, with the ziggurat, a massive steppe tower, symbolizing the mountain of the gods. The inner chamber, where the statue of Ishtar was kept, was the holiest area, accessible only to high priests and priestesses. The architecture of these temples facilitated the performance of rituals and ceremonies, to create an atmosphere where the divine, physical, and mortal worlds could connect and communicate.

Impact on Ancient Society

This evil and perverse worship engaged in by the priests and priestesses had a dark, infiltrating impact on ancient Mesopotamian society, shaping cultural, social, and political traditions. They believed that the rituals and ceremonies reinforced unity within the community, providing a shared set of beliefs and practices. Additionally, the temple and its priesthood played a significant role in the economic and administrative life of the city in which temples acted as centers of wealth and power. Ishtar also reinforced gender roles and sexuality, with her dual aspects of love and war demonically paving the way and empowering feminist ideology and power.

IMPACT ON TODAY'S CULTURE

I will begin speaking about Ishtar's impact on contemporary culture by explaining an encounter we had on a prayer assignment in April of 2023 in Germany. On this assignment, Holy Spirit clearly spoke concerning an antichrist agenda waiting to rise in the nations. As we continued in further research and prayer, we felt the Lord strongly directing us to pray at the Ishtar Gate that is housed in the Pergamonmuseum (Pergamon Museum).

The Ishtar Gate was constructed by the Babylonian King Nebuchadnezzar II circa 575 BC. It was the eighth gate of the city of Babylon (in present-day Iraq) and was the main entrance into the city. The Processional Way was used for the *akitu* New Year's celebration, through which statues of the deities would parade down and the path paved with red and yellow stones.[5]

Ishtar's Attempt at a New Temple

Whie driving to Berlin, the Lord began to speak to us to dig deeper in our research, that there was significant history we still needed to discover. As He usually does when He is trying to get our attention on a strategic issue, it was taking us an exceptionally long time to get to our destination—double the time. As we have learned to do in these situations, we engaged in intercession, seeking the Lord and listening to His guidance to hear and see what He was revealing.

We were an hour outside of Berlin, and the Lord told me to research a specific question. To be honest, I don't even remember what it was because of what was then discovered. Nonetheless, what He told me to type in the search engine is what led us to know what we know now but did not know then. I was taken to a website that began to speak of the Knights Templar who encountered an apparition of Isais who in turn revealed herself as Ishtar.

It was in the year 1220, the German Knight Templar and Commander Hubertus Koch along with a few companions were returning to Austria from the crusades. When they arrived at the ruins of Nineveh in ancient Babylon, he was approached by an apparition of a goddess Isais. She gave Koch instructions to return to the mountain of the Old God Wotan, also known as the Unterberg. He was charged with building a house there and given instruction to wait for her next apparition in which she would give crucial revelation concerning the new Golden Age for the world. In researching Assyrian history, Isais corresponds to the Assyrian goddess *Isai* who appeared in apparitions to the royal house.

In 1221, Koch arrived at the mountain and he set up his first command house. The remains of the wall sockets can still be seen in Marktschellenberg. The first testified and recorded apparition of Isais at Unterberg occurred in 1226. This began a repeated pattern of visitations over the next twelve years leading into 1238. In each of these encounters she delivered a demonic prophecy that culminated into 134 scribed verses. In one of the encounters, she gave an eight-sided black stone as a gift, and from that time Koch's unit of Knights Templar became known as *The Lords of the Black Stone* who are still in operation today.

Foundational to these Isais revelations is a heresy known as the Marcionite heresy. Marcion was the son of a bishop. In 135 AD, he was in Rome and developed heretical theological beliefs that soon turned into a cult espousing that the Hebrew God Jehovah was not the true God and He was not the Father of Jesus. Isais states that it was Allvater, God Himself who descended in human form and He Himself was Jesus, the one crucified. In German history, Allvater can also mean the demonic god Odin.

In one demonic visitation Isais explained that Ishtar is the intermediary for the Allvater and she is her secret aide. It is scribed in the revelations that Isais comes from the place called *kuthgracht,* "the dreadful chief abode of the demons, incomprehensible to all beings except the demons, whose greatness is of a kind that even God does not control" (Ilu-Asherah 4:12).[6] In her dark revelation she shares she has also been a demon but achieved the rank of goddess by her virtue.

She goes on to further reveal that the time of Ishtar/Isais will come, "When the Earth and the hearts of all the peoples shall enter the Golden Age perhaps in 1,000 years,"[7] meaning 1,000 years from the time of the demonic visitation in the 13th century. Before their "time" comes, Ishtar and Isais will lead the heroes (verse 94). She reveals at the center of Purgatory is the glorious fortress realm of Valhalla, where dwell the warrior gods with their wives (verse 15), the latter presumably being the *Valkyries* of Nordic legend: both Ishtar and Isais have right of hospitality there (verse 29).[8]

It is astounding and very sad to me the depth that lost mankind has been given over to the fascination with the occult and demonic realms. It is also alarming the degree to which these demonic entities are listened to and entertained. But sadly, many do this, thus welcoming increased demonic activity and empowerment. This is exactly what was transpiring with these German Knights. Isais continued to guide these men through demonic apparitions.

In 1235, acting on information received from her, German Templars Roderich and Emmerant visited Carthage in search of the missing writings of Marcion. The city of Carthage was a center of early Christianity in the second century. Byrsa was the name of a hill situated near the city. Within the hill was a grotto to Tanit, who had been the city goddess of Carthage. In this grotto the two Templars had an encounter with Ishtar. The following is Roderich's account:

> The apparition was a figure clothed in a breath-fine dress of shimmering green such that one could perceive the outline of a tall female…shining through it. She was…half woman and half girl, and undoubtedly not of this world…a golden tiara held back the masses of her hair, which reached to the ground; and on top of the tiara was a golden crescent moon with points like horns, and at its center a golden sun…She was translucent and not of humankind.
>
> She said, "I called you here without you being aware of it," at which Roderich asked for her identity. She answered at once, "I am Isai, Ishtar."
>
> Emmerant said that they were both true to the Lord Jesus Christ and would never worship another deity.

Ishtar apparently amused replied, "I heard your prayers to him, to my godlike brother. But he is in his realm while I, his godlike sister, am here again—for a short while. For ultimately it is female power which will defeat Jehovah, Satan. The goddess of love will change into a goddess of war to strike down Satan when the moment comes."

She continued: "You will find not far from this place an ancient stone which bears the sign of my divinity and the symbol of the hand in greeting. Beneath this stone you will discover that which you came here to find."

The goddess Ishtar stated next: "I had been appointed the deity for Babylon by the Godhead. The Babylonians were an excellent people but the settlement of a huge Hebrew minority in their midst ruined the plan to make Babylon the world capital." Ishtar explained that a people closest in character to the Babylonians, the Germanen including all the Franks of German descent, had been chosen to build a new capital "over a secret temple in which all your knowledge is to be deposited." Thus Berlin-Tempelhof was founded in 1237, and the new Templar realm was to extend south from Berlin to Vienna and as far west as Paris.[9]

Friends, allow me to state when I read this information out loud to the team, we were all shocked! Before continuing I want to state we love Germany, we love Berlin and the beautiful people of Germany. We had no idea that Berlin was established in the 1200s as Berlin Tempelhof (Temple) on the beliefs of the Knights Templar and Ishtar. We were also riled up in a righteous anger as Ishtar referred to Jehovah as satan. It is not a surprise a demonic principality would do this. It is expected from satan and demons. They are pure evil. But these Templars heeded her words, believed her, obeyed, acted on her instruction, and established the new location of her city temple in Berlin. And yes, Berlin was the Nazi world headquarters in World War II. And the infamous Berlin Tempelhof airport that was established by Hitler was intentionally built on these grounds where the original Knights Templar sanctuary and worship chapel was built. It is now very clear why the Lord kept saying dig deeper. In the 1200s Berlin was actually built and established by these Templars with the intent of it being the temple and dwelling place of Ishtar. It was time to shut the Ishtar Gate housed in the Pergamonmuseum!

When we arrived, we noticed poster advertising that a portion of the museum housing the seat of satan was temporarily closed until 2027 as it was under renovation. Preparations were underway for great plans in the near future. We viewed a virtual tour of what the museum was attempting to collect as part of their renowned exhibitions. To our disdain, it was a plan to secure and gain numerous ancient Babylonian gods, goddesses, and altars. We were literally seeing that this Ishtar Gate was the gate welcoming the convening together of all the ancient Babylonian gods, goddesses, altars, and cultures in this one location. Whether it is known or unknown by the people, from the 1200s throughout the history of Berlin, Ishtar has caused chaos and havoc to establish her demonic grip in that city and nation. Based off her demonic prediction, the "time of Ishtar" is approximately 200 years from now. This explains the need for the Ishtar Gate to be brought to Berlin. She must have it in her temple city as the procession way for her Golden Age New World and kingdom. Well, no thank you, Ishtar. Not going to happen on our watch!

Friends, it should not be hard to imagine this museum did not feel like a museum. Yes, many patrons visit the museum for no other reason than to learn about and view sites of ancient history. Spiritually, it was an active Babylonian gate and worship structure that was planned for world power. The day we prayed to shut down this Ishtar Gate and declare all power broken from this location was Sunday, April 23. Six months to the day after we prayed, on October 23, the entire museum was shut down due to the fact that it is sinking under the weight of these ancient Babylonian demonic systems and structures! They have stated that there is a 14-year plan costing millions of dollars to renovate the museum, but many are skeptical that this financial hurdle and restructuring feat will occur. And we stand in agreement that it won't!

FURTHER REVELATIONS OF HER AGENDA

I believe that this Ishtar Gate and the Pergamonmuseum sinking and being shut is the Lord resounding out that it is the time of the fulfilling of His judgment against this demonic entity. As His called and chosen warriors, we are in the anointed time to shut her demonic gates and to see her altars destroyed. It is time to dethrone Ishtar. I will share briefly further discoveries made in research following this assignment. It is plain to see that all Ishtar stood for in ancient Babylon, she has also attempted to release from Berlin into nations.

Before doing so, I want to state that each nation must investigate its own history and story. As I share a few more examples of how Ishtar brought her influence into nations from her so-called temple city, I pray that spiritual wisdom and understanding will be made known to see breakthrough in all nations where she is exerting her demonic power. I want to state emphatically that we love the people of Berlin and the city of Berlin. We are praying for a great move of the Lord in Berlin, Germany, Europe, and all the nations. This is why we pray on assignment, to see the enemy's schemes defeated and those in the region encounter victorious breakthrough, a harvest of souls, and Kingdom destiny realized. The Lord has an awesome purpose and plan for the people and nation of Germany. All that has been shared is a sinister, evil plan of a demonic principality, and trust me she is attempting the same in other nations. What I am discussing now is how Ishtar has manifested her schemes in my nation to establish her demonic kingdom within society and culture.

GOVERNMENTALLY

We see how Hitler and his Nazi army were drawn to Berlin for it to be their world headquarters. I will say the Lord of the Black Stones became the foundation of the occult German society called the Thule society. This occult group influenced Hitler and the Nazi ideology. You see, when those in leadership, in government, or those in power give themselves knowingly or unknowingly to sin or agree to align with a principality such as Ishtar, it opens the way—the gate—for principalities to be seated over the spiritual atmosphere and culture. Thus, their world headquarters was established at the Temple of Berlin. In other words, now that we have more understanding of the land and city that Ishtar tried to claim as her own, from there she attempted her world satanic takeover. Praise God this agenda through the Knights Templar, Hitler, and the Nazis was conquered!

History reports that Winston Churchill credits much of this victory to the intercession of a man by the name of Rees Howells and his prayer warriors. I realize there were many on their knees praying and interceding during that time. The Allied forces came together to defeat this demonic regime as well. All the while, at the Bible College of Wales, in the nation of Wales, was an anointed man, an intercessor called by the Lord. Rees Howells was completely surrendered to Holy Spirit in intercession for nations, along with a group of 120 prophetic intercessors. They prayed on call for years in obedience to the Lord to see the Nazi antichrist structure and all its occult empowerment completely defeated and conquered.

That being stated, we must see within our cities and nations how this ancient principality is tirelessly and diabolically perpetuating her agenda. Within the United States, there are many ways in which Ishtar has manifested. One of the most recent opened doors empowering this ancient principality's hold is the passing of legislation for same-sex marriage. As we have learned in the teaching concerning Ishtar, one of the driving forces is perversion, sexual identity confusion, transgender, and transvestite. On December 8, 2022:

> The House of Representatives on Thursday gave final approval to a landmark bill aimed at protecting same-sex and interracial marriage, sending the measure to President Joe Biden's desk for his signature.
>
> The final vote on the Respect for Marriage Act was 258-169, with 39 Republicans joining all Democrats to pass the measure. One Republican member voted "present."[10]

The legislation cleared Congress, sending it to President Biden to be signed into law and capping an improbable path for a measure that only months ago appeared to have little chance at enactment.

> President Joe Biden signed the Respect for Marriage Act into law on Tuesday, just a few days after the House passed the bill Respect for Marriage Act in 258-169 vote on Thursday. The historic bill repeals the Defense of Marriage Act and ensures that all states across the country will recognize same-sex marriages should the Supreme Court overturn Obergefell v. Hodges, a case that guaranteed the right to marriage for same-sex couples nationally in 2015.[11]

In fact, in the final weeks of writing this book, President Biden further empowered this entity. In previous years, March 31 had been designated by the President as the Transgender Day of Visibility. This year of writing this book, 2024, Easter Sunday (which many, including me, prefer to term Resurrection Day) occurred on this calendar date. Even so, his presidential statement affirming Transgender Day and those engaged in this lifestyle was released. This was a blatant and blasphemous act to declare the day of Jesus' resurrection as transgender day. This is a further empowerment of Ishtar in our nation. As a quick side note, we term it Resurrection Day, as the name Easter, itself, is associated with ancient forms of fertility goddess worship from ancient Mesopotamia and Europe.

SEXUAL PERVERSION

As has been shared, sexual perversion, sacred prostitution, and homosexuality were all part of the worship of the priests and priestesses in Ishtar's cult. She herself was transgender, sometimes a man and sometimes a woman. They were transvestites, and the gala castrated themselves and dressed as women to be of a higher class of priests and spiritual enlightenment and empowerment in her cult. Why am I rehearsing this information? Out of Berlin, the first ever recorded attempt at a sex change operation occurred in the year 1907.

I find it interesting that from Berlin there were several movements birthed through a homosexual man by the name of Dr. Magnus Hirschfeld. One of the movements being the Institute for Sexual Research. He and another doctor performed transgender surgeries on men, altering them to women. The first was Rudolf Richter, whose identity was changed to Dora Richter. The second was Einar Wegener, whose identity was changed to Lili Ebie, who died from infections shortly following his surgeries.

In World War II, the Nazis raided the clinic and burned most of the books, research, and writing. Hirschfeld had long before left Germany for world travel speaking about the homosexual lifestyle and transgender operations. His collaborator, Dr. Gohrbandt, joined the Luftwaffe as chief medical examiner and contributed to grim experiments in the Dachau concentration camp. It's interesting that Hirschfeld also was a proponent of eugenics, the feminist movement, and a strong voice for making abortion legal.

Dr. Harry Benjamin, an endocrinologist and sexologist from Berlin, was greatly influenced by Hirschfeld and the Institute for Sexual Research. He came to the US in 1913, eventually opening his own medical practice in New York. He was one of the doctors who worked with Christine Jorgensen, an American actress, singer, recording artist, and transgender activist who was the first person to become widely known in the United States for having sex reassignment surgery. Dr. Benjamin later worked with Reed Erickson, the founder and funder of the Erickson Educational Foundation, which published educational booklets and funded medical conferences, counseling services, the establishment of gender clinics, and the Harry Benjamin Foundation. Dr. Benjamin along the way became associated with Dr. John Money as they both worked with Johns Hopkins Hospital with funding provided by Reed Erickson. I don't have space in this book to fully discuss Dr. John Money. But he is now labeled as an evil pedophile. He was the doctor who held and perpetuated the belief that even if a boy was born a boy but nurtured to be a girl, he would be a girl—thus the phrase "nurture versus nature." His care and practice of this ideology resulted in the suicidal deaths of twin boys Brian and David Reimer.

Dr. Benjamin and Dr. Money both worked closely with Dr. Albert Kinsey, a sexologist who founded the Institute for Sex Research at Indiana University with studies steeped in pure evil, perversion, and pedophilia. To share a big praise report! After years of focused intercession and activism, this Institute lost its state funding although it is not been fully shut down as of yet.

These doctors and their voices pushed the thinking and mindsets of many, perpetuating the Ishtar agenda concerning the belief in a third gender, nurture versus nature, and pedophilia acts that condone practices and experiments on young children under the guise of medical practice. This has impacted our nation. This principality Ishtar has now been established through same-sex marriage legalization and surgeries to transition genders; it is flooding our education system and attempting to take our next generation through their teaching in public schools. The most grievous is the influence within the Christian Church. Same-sex marriage is now welcomed and accepted in many Christian denominations and non-denominational churches and ministries. It is time to come out from her!

A GATE TO EMPOWER WICCA AND FEMINISM

It is evident that this ancient principality is still very active. Let take a moment and give further insight to another open door further welcoming Ishtar's evil hold. Witchcraft in all its many forms has grown exponentially in our nation. One form that is greatly widespread is Wicca. It is the largest of modern pagan and neo-pagan religions. Its followers typically identify as witches who find their inspiration from pre-Christian religions of Europe. The pentagram or five-pointed star is often used as their main symbol.

It spread rapidly from England throughout the United States during the countercultural intellectual and moral climate of the 1960s and 1970s and the social movements of that period. A connection between Wicca and feminism has developed during what is termed the second wave feminist movement. Those engaged in second wave Wicca beliefs see the witch as misunderstood yet a powerful female traditional practitioner. Dianic Wicca focused on the spiritual connection with the goddess Diana. It was formed in 1971. It drew on the gay rights movement forming its own brotherhood for gay and bisexual men. The growing environmentalist sentiment also had great impact on Wicca, which also began to call itself a nature religion. The following quote brings clarity.

> But in all cases, goddess worship has been described as a direct political protest against a misogynistic, mainstream, environmentally destructive, god-worshipping society. In short, modern American feminists have created a domestic and politically charged spiritual practice called goddess worship.[12]

Sadly, one location that is considered sacred and holy to Wiccans is the Statue of Liberty. To give a brief history, the statue was built by Freemasons from France, Gustave Ellis and Frederic Auguste Bartholdi, and funded from the resources of this society.

> Bartholdi sailed to America in 1871 to make arrangements for the presentation of the monument on July 4, 1876. …Upon approaching America, it is said he had a vision of a goddess holding a torch in one hand, welcoming visitors to the land of freedom and opportunity. This vision would become the first sketch of the Statue of Liberty…[whose purpose is to] light the way to freedom peacefully and lawfully. And so the name, "Liberty Enlightening the World," was bestowed upon the yet-to-be-made statue.[13]

History tells that the goddess Bartholdi saw in his vision was the Roman goddess Libertas. When researching Libertas, her foundation is birthed out of Ishtar.

President Grover Cleveland had this to say at the Statue of Liberty's dedication on October 28, 1886:

> We are not here today to bow before the representative of a fierce and war-like god, filled with wrath and vengeance, but, instead, we contemplate our own peaceful deity keeping watch before the open gates of America, and greater than all that have been celebrated in ancient song. Instead of grasping in her hand the thunderbolts of terror and of death, she holds aloft the light that illumines the way to man's enfranchisement.[14]

It is wonderful that there is a deep place in the hearts of the American people, including me, to express the great importance of the freedoms that have been given and bestowed in this nation. I absolutely love our nation and I am so grateful for the foundations of our Christian faith in this nation. We pray for great revival and awakening in our nation and all nations. Often sentiments and gratitude for the blessing of freedom are shown in building memorials, landmarks in honor of this freedom, which is absolutely a wonderful expression and should be done. However, building a statue of a goddess and positioning it as a gateway into the nation is unfortunately a red carpet welcome mat for that goddess to have a demonic hold in the land. Whether he did so knowingly or unknowingly is not mine to judge. The truth is many are unaware of the spiritual ramifications that certain actions incur. That being said, President Cleveland opened a demonic gate by inaugurating Lady Liberty as America's goddess, America's peaceful deity, and further declaring her greater than all other gods. Her influence has not diminished in this nation to this day with those who choose to view and worship her as a goddess. Allow me to explain.

On the website *Circle Sanctuary*, Selena Fox clearly reveals the goddess status of Lady Liberty within their pagan worship and belief.

> To many contemporary Wiccans and other Pagans, Lady Liberty is more than a symbol. She is a powerful and ancient Goddess who can guide, inspire, protect, and comfort. Pagans have invoked Lady Liberty in rituals for personal and/or social liberation. Some Pagans include Her image in their household shrines and altars.[15]

Many occult groups such as Wiccans are encouraged to pray to the statue of Liberty and engage in ceremonial prayers and rituals.

> On a symbolically important day such as a patriotic holiday or a seasonal Sabbat, leave an offering at (or in alignment with) the feet of a statue or picture of Liberty. The offering can be a flower, a coin, a special stone or crystal, or something that signifies "freedom" to you. Sit or stand quietly before Her image, and pray through it to the Goddess it represents. From then on, whenever you feel so moved, or whenever you pass by the image, send forth a prayer for freedom. You can pray for liberation from any unjust oppression, whether personal or collective—"free me," or "free us."[16]

The majority of us in America would not look to worship or engage in any type of prayer to the Statue of Liberty nor have thoughts in that direction. We see it as a symbol of our freedoms and liberties, which we are all so grateful for and rejoice in. These Wiccan practices of the worship of Lady Liberty welcome and empower the evil grip of the goddess of Ishtar and Diana and the spread of pagan worship in New York and across the nation. And friends, we know the One of all truth. Our Heavenly Father is the sovereign One who brings peace. No goddess will ever accomplish this.

HOW TO RESPOND

Friends, I could continue to share research concerning Ishtar. Several more chapters could be written. I am sharing key points to help in understanding the many ways this ancient principality has and is still establishing its demonic grip in our nation and nations. More research and prophetic insight could be shared. In closing, below is a personal prayer for freedom for those who feel they would like to pray and shut all open doors, and, it's also a sample prayer of how to pray strategically.

Personal Prayer

Father, thank You for Your truth that sets me free. Jesus, thank You that by Your blood and through Your Name I'm forgiven, cleansed, and set free. Holy Spirit, thank You for Your presence and anointing for freedom and victory.

I now confess and repent for myself and previous generations in my family bloodline concerning all involvement and engagement in or with the beliefs, worship, or practices of Ishtar. I repent and ask that You forgive me for all sexual perversion in my life including activities, beliefs supporting all forms of idolatry, and perversion in alignment with Ishtar. I repent for adultery, prostitution, homosexuality, lesbianism, cross-dressing, pedophilia, pornography, child pornography, and any financial funding toward these acts of perversion. I repent for all involvement in paganism, Wicca, occult practices, witchcraft practices, and sex magic that I and my family bloodline have participated in. I repent for all thoughts and activity of witchcraft, rebellion, goddess worship, and ideologies of feminism.

Jesus, thank You that by Your blood and through Your name I am now cleansed and forgiven.

I now renounce perversion, homosexuality, lesbianism, child pornography, prostitution, sex magic, transgender beliefs and practices, all agreement with transvestite activities and ideologies. I renounce the financial curse that has come with the funding of all of these sins of perversion. I break your hold in my life and I command you to go now.

I renounce all witchcraft, Wicca, and occult practices. I renounce all idolatry, worship, and perverse sex magic and command you to get out of my life now.

I renounce all mindsets of and agreement with activities of witchcraft, rebellion, and goddess empowerment through the ungodly agenda of the feminist movement and I command you to get out of my life now!

Father, thank You for Your freedom and victory. I rejoice that I am free and free indeed! Holy Spirit, every place where my house has been swept clean, fill me up to overflowing. I welcome and declare purity and holiness in my thoughts, mind, emotions, and desires. I declare that Your Word is alive in me. I ask for more of You in my life. Jesus, You are the Alpha, Omega, the Beginning and the End. You are the Magnificent One, the Holy One, the Redeemer of the World. You are Holy. All glory, power, and honor are due Your name,

and I say that You are the One True Magnificent King.
I rejoice in You, Lord!

Research Guidelines for Informed Intercession

For those who want to engage in research in your region, spheres of influence, or prayer assignments the Lord is highlighting, I am including questions at the end of several chapters. These questions are guideposts and tools to give direction in the research process. This is referred to as spiritual mapping and defined as the process of combining prophetic revelation with historical research that provides a map to effectively discern and implement strategies of breakthrough. Remember, this is a guide to help initiate the process. Friends, while engaging in this mapping process, it is so key to release glory-anointed worship in the region, to steadfastly intercede for revival and awakening, and to stand tenacious in seeing His prophetic fulfillment and destiny break forth. Keep the fires burning in personal and corporate intercession. Be expectant and faith filled for victorious breakthrough and awakening transformation. You too can see demonic gates shut and glory portals open in your spheres of influence and regions.

Chapter Nine will be completely dedicated to the structure of the Knights Templar written by my friend Brandon Larson. Therefore, I will only direct a couple of questions below in that direction and save the others for that chapter.

1. Are there medical practices in your region that perform sex-change operations?

2. Are there universities in the region that train doctors on how to perform sex-change operations?

3. Are the Masonic orders strongly emphasizing the Order of the Knights Templar?

4. Is there a strong homosexual, lesbian, transgender community in your region/sphere of influence?

5. Are government leaders or key influencers in your region engaging in sexually perverse acts?

6. Have local government leaders, business leaders, church leaders endorsed and supported the LGBTQ agenda? If so, has identificational repentance occurred?

7. Are transvestites and transgenders welcome to speak in the public schools in the region?

8. Are there witchcraft covens or Wiccans in the region who are involved in the spheres of influence?

9. What other forms of witchcraft and the occult are in operation?

10. How active are these occult groups?

11. Is the feminist movement active in your region or sphere of influence?

12. Are these groups engaged in the schools and education system?

13. What are the prophetic and redemptive promises of the Lord?

14. What are His Kingdom strategies of stewardship of those words?

15. Have there been past moves of revival? If so, pray in agreement that those wells of revival will be awakened again.

16. How is the Lord moving now? Identify those areas and pray in agreement with the moves of His Spirit. Intercede for more of His glorious presence, for revival and awakening.

17. Intercede for revival and awakening in the churches and spheres of culture and influence.

Chapter Five

LILITH

In 1994, I had a series of dreams in which the Lord opened my spiritual sight revealing the demonic spiritual entity Lilith. He did so to release revelation and understanding in the ways in which this principality operates. It was a three-week period of revelation in which I was literally spying on the night witch demon (one of her many names) in the spirit realm. Yet she remained totally unaware. Why was this occurring?

Chuck Pierce had given a prophetic word concerning the city of Houston. He saw that the night hag, also a name for Lilith, was singing over the city in an attempt to establish a stronghold. He gave the directive that the intercessors had three weeks to thwart this demonic assignment. In the series of dreams, the Lord expressly showed me this territorial deity to be one of the principal forces behind death and abortion. The most poignant dream revealed a key revelation and strategy for intercession that we have implemented since that time as led by the Lord.

In the dream, Greg and I were driving in a car with Alice Smith, a dear friend and mentor in my life. We were on the way to a church picnic being held on a country farm. As we arrived, Greg parked the car in an open space. Alice and I exited the car. Suddenly, we saw a black bull charging toward us. This bull was angry and coming with the full intention to gore and kill us. Alice and I instantly in unison stomped our feet and commanded the bull to stop. He came to an abrupt halt. The bull then stood up on its hind hoofs. With his front right foot, the bull reached behind the back of his head and began to unzip a zipper. It was clear that the body of the black bull was a costume. As the bull costume fell to the ground out stepped Lilith. I then heard the Lord say, "In order to see breakthrough with Baal structures, you must deal with Lilith. She is the one disguising and hiding herself yet wielding the power of seduction and death." This provides further revelation concerning demonic principalities and what we learned when studying Ishtar—principalities are androgynous and do appear in different manifestations across cultures.

HISTORY OF LILITH

Lilith is cited in Isaiah 34:14, *"The wild beasts of the desert shall also meet with the wild beasts of the island, and the satyr shall cry to his fellow; the screech owl also shall rest there, and find for herself a place of rest"* (KJV). The Hebrew word is *lilim*, with the English version being *Lilith*, whose name means the night monster, night hag, or screeching owl (Strong's #H8163). This ancient principality has appeared in demonic witchcraft beliefs, demonic sexual encounters, and the death of infants from the foundation of time to modern history. Her origins are from Babylonian and Assyrian mythology, but she was also identified in later Jewish legends as a night hag, screeching owl, night monster demon. Let's go into a brief overview of her evil and deceptive manifestations throughout history and culture to gain revelation and wisdom on how she is actively entrenched in society today.

EPIC OF GILGAMESH

Lilith first appears in 2000 BC in secular Babylonian literature within the ancient Sumerian narrative, "Gilgamesh and the Huluppu Tree" (sometimes called the willow tree), originally written on clay tablets as a sequence of poems. It is interesting that this story was initially titled "Innana and the Huluppu Tree," which we discussed in Chapter Four. The text was inscribed across multiple tablets. Remnants still survive today containing the Semitic language of Babylon. In the tale she is identified as the evil demon Lillake. Her legend reveals that she dwelled in the trunk of a willow tree tended by Innana (Ishtar) on the bank of the Euphrates from the beginning of Creation. From this era and still today, many of her devotees believe that Lilith was the serpent in the tree of the knowledge of good and evil in the Garden of Eden that deceived Eve. Her demonic cohorts are a dragon nesting at the base of the tree and Anzu, an evil god whose offspring nest on the height of the tree. The epic hero Gilgamesh intervenes, killing the dragon with his immense bronze ax. Overcome by terror, Lilith demolishes her abode and escapes into the wilderness.

JEWISH LORE AND THE ORIGINS OF LILITH

In Rabbinic and Jewish lore, the creation story of Genesis occurs in chronological order. They translate the creation account in

Genesis 1 and 2 to be divided into two parts that seem to counter-act each other. In the familiar narrative of Genesis 2, God forms Adam first and subsequently creates Eve from Adam's rib, intend-ing for her to be Adam's companion and helper. Lilith's appearance in the Book of Genesis still stands as one of the most controversial mentions in religious texts, and rightfully so. In the brief account in Genesis 1 the Jewish mystic legend believes there was a simul-taneous creating of both a man and a woman in God's likeness from the same soil per their interpretation of Genesis 1:27, *"So God created mankind in his own image, in the image of God he cre-ated them; male and female he created them"* (NIV). Therefore, they find a distinct difference between the two accounts of creation, providing their foundational belief that Lilith was Adam's initial spouse, equally fashioned from the earth alongside him. Eve, then, emerges as Adam's subsequent wife and the forebearer or mother of humankind. Although Lilith is never mentioned by name in this scripture, in Jewish mythology she is broadly recognized as Adam's first wife and, by extension, the first woman ever created.

The Dead Sea Scrolls

Lilith also appears in the Dead Sea Scrolls, which are ancient manuscripts, mostly Hebrew, discovered beginning in 1947 in the caves of Qumran on the northwestern shore of the Dead Sea. Lilith is mentioned among demons, howlers, and desert bandits that God protects against. Below she is called out by name in the Song of the Sage, a hymn used in exorcisms.

> And I, the Sage, sound the majesty of His beauty to ter-rify and confound all the spirits of destroying angels… the demons, Lilith…and those that strike suddenly, to

lead astray the spirit of understanding, and to make desolate their heart.[1]

The Talmud

The Talmud is a compilation of legal discussions, stories of rabbis, and commentaries on Bible passages that have become a central source for Jewish religious law and theology. In the Talmud, Lilith is mentioned in different contexts. She is cited and established within the Jewish scholarly world as the demonic entity she truly is, the mother of the demons. Further mentions from Babylonian demonology depict her as a nocturnal great-winged goddess with bird-clawed feet. She carries a ring or rod of power, signifying that she is among the first-ranked gods. She is a seductress, replete with destruction, known as the goddess of death or Hades. She is one of a triad mentioned in Babylonian magic spells and shares common traits with the following demonic entities: the Ardat Lili, a lustful female who attacks single men; Labratu, a female demon with wild hair that kills children and sucks their blood, and yes, this serves as the foundation of belief in vampirism; and Lilitu, a female spirit or wind demon as she is referenced in a seventh-century Assyrian inscription in which authority over her is being declared, "Oh flyer of dark chamber go at once oh lily."[2] Praise God! We agree! Lilith leave at once!

The Alphabet of Ben Sira

After long periods of time with few mentions, Lilith begins to ensure her enthronement is entrenched in ideology and seated firmly over culture as shared in a manuscript titled The Alphabet of Ben Sira. It is a text of Jewish folklore that contains a demonic satirical mocking tone to biblical stories. Lilith becomes the central focus in the fifth stanza.

Here she is also spoken of as the woman who was Adam's first wife who refuses to lie submissively beneath him in relations between a man and woman. She rebels against God and Adam. Invoking the unmentionable name of God, she sins and is supernaturally empowered to sprout wings, enabling her to fly from the Garden of Eden to the Red Sea in Egypt. Her dramatic departure reestablishes for a new generation Lilith's supernatural character as a winged devil. Here to fulfill her lewd desires she began to engage with demons birthing hundreds of demons daily. Hence her identity as mother of demons. God sent three angels to bring her back. She refused, stating she was the one who was to be the devourer of children. God judged her, killing 100 of her demon children daily. She then began perverse night attacks against Adam in his dreams.

In this demonic and perverse depiction, she becomes identified as a shape-shifter, which is the ability to appear in any form she wants, human or animal. She is a seductress and the one who birthed the spirits of incubus and succubus. Incubus is a demon in male form that appears to women in dreams with the evil agenda of seduction or rape. Succubus is a demon in female form that appears to a man in his dreams with the evil agenda of seduction or rape. In my 34 years of experience in deliverance ministry, the casting out of spirits of succubus and incubus occurs quite frequently. I have also ministered to several coming out of shamanism who speak of Lilith and her evil ability to empower their shape-shifting occult activities.

In ancient beliefs all the way to modern witchcraft beliefs and occult witchcraft circles, it is believed that this dark entity has charge over all newborn infants, with the satanic assignment to strangle and kill. This was so entrenched in Jewish occult mysticism that amulets would be placed on the outside wall of birthing rooms to ward off Lilith. For infant boys, the amulet would be left until his eighth day of life, the day of circumcision. For the girls it would remain on the wall for twelve days following birth.

Book of Zohar and the Kabballah

Believed to have been written in Spain by Moses de Leon (1250–1305), *The Book of Zohar* serves as the foundational literature of mystical and occult thought known as the Kabbalah. It brings in another spin on the biblical tale of creation. This demonic lie states that in the Genesis 1:27 account the first created human was androgynous—half man, being Adam, and half woman, being Lilith. God eventually severed and separated the two. Eve is created and Lilith is enraged in jealousy and anger and flees the Garden of Eden to begin her evil acts. Here her demonic sway to be identified as the first feminist begins to evolve.

CONTINUING HER EVIL AGENDA

As we see, Lilith has diabolically secured her demonic grip throughout time and history. In European folklore she sits as the presiding goddess of the Witches' Sabbat and the female leader of the Wild Hunt. She is identified with Medusa who kills men with her deadly gaze, the harpy who shrieks in the night, Lamia who devours her lovers, and other bloodthirsty demonic manifestations. In occult and witchcraft, she is known as the baby-killing witch. Understanding that she desires this evil agenda, ancient lullabies were derived from *lilith abi,* which actually is Hebrew for "Lilith be gone." To guard against Lilith, Jewish mothers would hang four amulets on the nursery walls with the inscriptions "Lilith aby" or "Lilith be gone." Her legend continues to serve as a source of material in modern Western culture literature, occultism, fantasy, horror, movies, comic books, online games. Let's all agree together in the name of Jesus that this is the era of Lilith be gone!

MODERN OCCULTISM

Now let's move into modern occultism. This demon Lilith continues to be popular among Wiccans and modern occultists. Lilith appears as a succubus in Aleister Crowley's Diarte Magica. Aleister Crowley is known as one the most renowned occultists, a magician, an anti-Christian messiah, drug fiend, and sex addict. Lilith was also one of the middle names of Aleister Crowley's first child. Her full name was Nuit Ma Ahathoor Hecate Sappho Jezebel Lilith. But she went by Lilith. Sadly, she died from typhoid at two years of age, born in 1904 and died in 1906. This so breaks my heart for this precious baby and definitely stirs up a righteous indignation!

I do not find it a coincidence that one of Crowley's first occult initiations was into the Hermetic Order of the Golden Dawn that occurred in Berlin, Germany. This order was rooted in the occult practices and beliefs stemming from the German Knights Templar mentioned in Chapter Four, but it was officially founded and named in 1887 by three British Freemasons. It admits freely to being an initiatory society devoted to spiritual, philosophical, and magical development; ritual divination, including the Kabballah; and occult sciences. They claimed that the order was guided in part by what they named the Secret Chiefs or the Concealed Rulers of the Wisdom of the True Rosicrucian. Many believed the Secret Chiefs were alchemists whose lineage began in Ancient Egypt. "Indeed, many of the Golden Dawn's rituals involved the invocation of Egyptian gods such as Horus, while the first Temple in London was named 'Isis-Urania,' the first part of which is the name of the Egyptian goddess of nature and magic."[3] Isis will be discussed in the next chapter.

Crowley was also initiated into another German-based occult group, the Ordo Templi Orientis (O.T.O.) eventually rising to become the leader of the British branch. Jack Parsons was an American rocket engineer and chemist who was one of the founders of NASA's Jet Propulsion Laboratory (JPL) and Aerojet Engineering Corporation. He was the first to invent the rocket. He was a known occultist under the tutelage of Crowley and established the Ordo Templi Orientis in the state of California. He and L. Ron Hubbard engaged in very dark, black magic and deviant magic rituals. They intentionally dedicated several months to very specific occult, perverse activities of which I will not go into detail. The purpose was to incarnate an actual goddess on earth. Their friendship severed when L. Ron Hubbard stole $20,000 from Parsons and ran off with his girl-friend. L. Ron Hubbard then founded the Church of Scientology having great impact in Hollywood.

Many occult writers and occultists attribute the modern-day Wicca movement as an honored place to invoke and worship Lillith. Numerous incantations and demonic occult rituals call-ing on and conjuring up Lilith are engaged in. She is invoked for demonic lewd and perverse encounters and is depicted by the symbols of a serpent, owl, crescent moon on top of a cross, black moon, and the grand seal of Lilith just to name a few.

MODERN PSYCHOLOGY

Carl Jung was a Swiss psychiatrist and psychoanalyst. While he himself did not extensively explore Lilith in his writings, some contemporary Jungian psychologists have explored the archetype of Lilith and its relevance to the psyche, particularly in relation to feminine aspects, the shadow self, and aspects of the anima. Jung's concept of the anima espouses the feminine aspects within the male psyche. This demon of Lilith has infiltrated into the realm psychology, particularly in relation to gender, sexuality, and the psyche.

BOHEMIAN GROVE

The Bohemian Grove is a private men's club located in Monte Rio, California. From the time of its establishment in 1872, it has become known for its secretive annual gatherings, attended by many prominent figures from politics, business, arts and entertainment, media education, etc. Many of our presidents and the world's wealthiest businessmen and influencers attend. Membership is $25,000 annually. Women are not allowed. They discuss national issues in the midst of a two-week party in which drinking, music, and prostitution are reported.

One of the most iconic symbols associated within the Bohemian Grove is the "Owl Shrine" or "Owl of Bohemia." The Owl Shrine is a large concrete sculpture of an owl, standing approximately 40 feet tall, located within the grove's grounds surrounded by redwood trees. It was designed by sculptor and artist Haig Patigian in the early 1920s and was constructed in 1929. Patigian also served as president of the club for many years.

The significance of the owl within the context of the Bohemian Grove is somewhat mysterious and has given rise to various interpretations. Some suggest that the owl represents wisdom, knowledge, or enlightenment, while others have associated it with ancient mythology and occult symbolism used in ancient Babylonian demon worship and druid witchcraft divination. A demonic ritual called the Cremation of Care was initiated in 1881. High priests call on the wisdom of the goddess (the owl) and place an effigy of a human body on the black altar positioned in front of the owl. The effigy is set on fire as a sacrifice. During his lifetime, Walter Cronkite played the voice of the owl in this ceremony. Friends, this is demonic and it is disturbing that world influencers engage in this type of ceremonial empowerment of Lilith.

FEMINISM

Lilith has become the icon driving the feminist movement. For example, Lilith Magazine was founded in 1976 by Susan Weidman Schneider, a journalist and activist. The magazine takes its name from Lilith, who has been embraced by feminists as a symbol of female empowerment and independence. The Lilith Fund was founded in 2001 by a group of activists in Texas who recognized the need for financial assistance for individuals who could not afford the cost of abortion care. Since its inception, the organization has been committed to providing direct financial support to people seeking abortions, as well as engaging in advocacy efforts to protect and expand abortion access in Texas and beyond.

The predominant manifestations of Lilith's significance in the feminist movement are telling. The movement highly promotes rebellion against patriarchy and believes in the demonic spiritual empowerment of women through:

1. The symbol of female empowerment.
2. Exploration of female sexuality.
3. The critique of traditional religious narratives.

The following is written by one activist in the feminist movement,

> Lilith's story really resonates with us, doesn't it? She's like this ancient beacon of strength that's been shining all the way through history to now, touching everything from old myths to the heart of today's fight for women's rights. She's not just a name or a character; she's become this icon for standing up against the old-school rules about who women should be. You can see her influence everywhere—in the art we admire, the books we get lost in, and the shows we binge-watch. She's that voice inside that whispers, "Be bold, be free!" …For anyone out there who's ever felt the need to break free and claim their space in the world, Lilith's spirit is like a guiding star…. Lilith has progressed from a legendary figure to an influential feminist icon. …By appreciating Lilith's rebellious nature, women are taking back their autonomy and disputing social conventions.[4]

I believe Janet Howe Gaines makes an accurate assessment concerning this demonic principality and her demonic scheme throughout the generations:

> Lilith's peregrinations continue today. This winged night creature is, in effect, the only "surviving" she-demon from the Babylonian empire, for she is reborn each time her character is reinterpreted. The retellings of the myth of Lilith reflect each generation's views of the feminine role. As we grow and change with the millennia, Lilith survives because she is the archetype for the changing role of woman.[5]

ABORTION

No one in his right mind would want to rehabilitate the reputations of Stalin, Mussolini, or Hitler. Their barbarism, treachery, and debauchery will make their names live on in infamy forever. Amazingly though, Sanger has somehow escaped their wretched fate. In spite of the fact that her crimes against humanity were no less heinous than theirs, her place in history has effectively been sanitized and sanctified. In spite of the fact that she openly identified herself in one way or another…with Stalin's Sobornostic Collectivism, with Hitler's Eugenic Racism, and with Mussolini's Agathistic Fascism.[6]

Margaret Sanger, known as a reformer, is responsible for the death of over 60 billion babies worldwide. Sanger's commitment to humanist progressivism positioned birth control as a cornerstone of an advanced society by effectively rendering the act of killing infants obsolete. Her viewpoint was shaped under the challenging and difficult conditions of her family life and further molded through interactions with some of the leading Darwinists of the twentieth century. Her personal and romantic involvement with H.G. Wells further solidified her ideological ties to Charles Darwin. Sanger was an activist of social evolution as the primary catalyst for change in the world, following its principles to their fullest extent. While her ideologies were initially viewed as extreme, they have since been welcomed on a global scale, effectively leaving her significant yet horrific mark on society.

At the age of nineteen, Margaret watched her mother die of tuberculosis. Her mother was a Catholic and her father, Michael Higgins, was an atheist. He was a Civil War veteran and known as a free-thinking socialist. He sparsely provided for the family by chiseling tombstones for local cemeteries. Margaret's mother conceived eighteen times with only eleven births. She describes her father's socialist radicalism as her foundation for her beliefs and actions.

She recalls one time at the age of nine being terribly sick with typhoid. She was barely coherent but awoke to her father lying on top of her in the act of abuse, noting this was her first time of awakening. Her father's extreme beliefs and behaviors were not limited to radical socialism and sexual violations. Margaret's brother Henry died at the age of four. She recalls her father taking her on a late-night visit to the cemetery where he dug up her brother's corpse, making a plaster mold of his head and shoulders to give to his wife as a gift. Friends, this just leaves me speechless. Undoubtedly, these sad and tragic events left dark and lingering psychological, emotional, and spiritual imprints.

Following her mother's passing, Sanger resumed her nursing career in the poverty-stricken Lower East Side of New York City, an area of the city with dire health and living conditions which she found deeply appalling. In 1912, the desperate circumstances of a young woman who sought help to end her pregnancy and consequently died from a botched abortion profoundly impacted Sanger. This tragic experience incited and secured her resolve to address what she felt was the overwhelming suffering of mothers. She was convinced that birth control, a phrase she is credited with inventing, was essential to addressing these moral crises.

The loss of her five-year-old daughter, Peggy, to pneumonia in 1915 grievously affected Sanger, leading her into years of spiritual searching marked by dreams of infant girls and subsequent reported communications with Peggy via occult practices and seances. Peggy's death drove Sanger into exploring Rosicrucianism, an occult spiritual movement emphasizing mystical dimensions of personal spiritual encounters through meditative practices aimed at discovering the god within. Rosicrucianism was steeped in the practices of Kabbalah in which the goddess of the Black Moon, Lilith, was invoked along with other gods and goddesses. Influenced by the secular and anti-Christian views of her father, Sanger was lacking a solid moral framework, pushing her toward secular and occult strategies in her advocacy for birth control.

In the 1920s, Sanger fell under the influence of several radical thinkers, social anarchists, and activists. As stated above, one was H.G. Wells, a radical Darwinist. Another, Emma Goldman, a feminist political anarchist. And Havelock Ellis, a sex psychologist who considered himself the messiah of sexual behaviors. He co-authored the first medical textbook on homosexuality in 1897 and served as one of the 16 vice presidents of the Eugenics Society. *Eugenics* is defined as, "the selection of desired heritable characteristics in order to improve future generations, typically in reference to humans…[it] advocated a system that would allow 'the more suitable races or strains of blood a better chance of prevailing speedily over the less suitable.'"[7] Margaet had an illicit affair with Ellis as she and her first husband, William Sanger, chose to be in an open marriage. She herself became a proponent of eugenics, which became a strong pillar belief of her birth control ideology and Planned Parenthood.

> In promoting birth control, she advanced a controversial "Negro Project," wrote in her autobiography about speaking to a Ku Klux Klan group and advocated for a eugenics approach to breeding for "the gradual suppression, elimination and eventual extinction, of defective stocks — those human weeds which threaten the blooming of the finest flowers of American civilization."[8]

Sadly, all of these ideologies became greatly exalted by Adolf Hiter and Joseph Goebbels. In 1934, Goebbels stated, "Margaret Sanger is the best National Socialist in America." Much of the Nazi ideology and laws created in their regime concerning racial cleansing was adopted by the ideas they had learned though the eugenics movement and Margaret Sanger. This led to the August 18, 1939 decree in which the Reich Ministry of Interior circulated a decree requiring all physicians, nurses, and midwives to report newborn infants and children under the age of three who showed signs of severe mental or physical disability. These children were brought to children's clinics and euthanized.

This leads to where we are now in the history of abortion with the RU486, also called the abortion pill. The German drug company used by the Nazis in World War II was sold to another German company, which in turn was bought by the French pharmaceutical company that is responsible for the creation and medical trial runs of the RU486 chemical abortion pill—a pill that medically and chemically aborts a baby. Now with a prescription in hand, a woman can purchase a pill and go through the process of chemical abortion in her home. It is dangerous and several have died. Thus ever empowering Lilith, the principality of death who kills future generations.

A most recent manifestation of Lilith caused a great stir. A new online abortion clinic was launched in February of 2023. The name—Samuel Alito's Mom's Satanic Abortion Clinic. Sadly, this is for real. I would not recommend visiting the site. They state their mission as a clinic is to provide religious medication abortion care, and even go as far as giving steps of how to ensure the abortion process is a spiritual one by welcoming and invoking demonic spirits and satan. *Cosmopolitan* magazine was active in the promotion of this clinic. This is pure evil, occult at the highest level, and blatant, all-out satanism.

It's time to declare, "But *God!*" Now is the time to conquer and dethrone this demonic principality!

LILITH IS CONQUERED!

My first trip into the state of Kansas was in 2005. I was invited in by recognized apostles Sandy Newman and DeeAnn Ward. They asked me to teach a group of hungry and attentive intercessors, pastors, and leaders who were fully prepared to study the importance of spiritual mapping and spiritual warfare. To my delight in the first teaching session, it was observable that the Lord had placed me with a passionate army of believers who were prepared to begin this journey of spiritual mapping, welcoming prophetic revelation from the throne room, and who were passionate about setting into action warfare strategies to see social transformation realized.

Wichita, Kansas, housed an abortion clinic run by a doctor who was viewed by the public and self-proclaimed as America's most prolific abortionist, Dr. George Tiller. In his lifetime vocation, he aborted no fewer than sixty thousand unborn infants.[9] Abortions, including late-term abortions, were the only medical procedures he executed in his practice. Sandy, DeeAnn, and others whom I was training felt strongly that the Lord was guiding them to contend with this death structure.

Since the initial training, I have returned to Kansas repeatedly. The trip in the fall of 2007 proved to be a divinely appointed and engineered strategic-level spiritual warfare assignment. For months, believers in the state had been aggressively researching and praying that the spiritual root or demonic principality behind the notorious abortion clinic would be exposed. And another organization, Operation Rescue, held three prayer initiatives in front of Tiller's clinic throughout the year of 2007. There was much focused prayer, but we knew that the principality itself needed to be uncovered and defeated in order to issue the final blow to ensure the closing of this clinic.

In preparation for our coming prophetic act, Sandy, DeeAnn, and I met with Stephanie Norton, their lead intercessor and researcher, and we prayed, asking the Lord to disclose the stronghold. At that moment, the Lord remarkably brought back to my memory the dream I had in 1994, which I shared in the opening of this chapter.

As I shared this revelation we all felt strongly that this was the principality perpetuating death through this abortion clinic. The next day they drove me to the airport for my return flight home. We decided to stop in front of the clinic to pray. A few minutes into the prayer, I heard the voice of the Lord, "Becca, bind Lilith now!" At the same exact time Sandy and DeeAnn heard the Lord speaking this as well. With all three of us in agreement, I spoke out, "In the name of Jesus I bind the territorial spirit of death. I bind you, Lilith, and say you no longer will be able to execute bloodshed of the innocent and unborn from this location. You will no longer advance in your demonic strategies and agendas. You are bound!"

After my flight departed and as Sandy and DeeAnn made their journey home, a fierce windstorm blew across the state. Two days later, Sandy and her staff returned to the church offices only to come upon an amazing surprise. In the only tree on the church property an owl was bound with fishing line used to hang decorations. They called a wildlife ranger to the church to free the owl. The key point to remember is that Lilith is characterized as the screeching owl!

Upon freeing the owl and examining it, the ranger told Sandy, "Based on the level of dehydration and the amount of bird waste below the tree, I can establish a fair estimate of how long the owl has been here. Do you recall the windstorm that blew across the state two days ago? I believe the wind made it impossible for the owl to fly and forcefully blew it into the tree where the fishing line bound it." Sandy immediately called me, "Becca, one hour after you prayed and bound Lilith who is the screeching owl demonic entity of death, the Lord sent a sign. Through a fierce windstorm, an owl was blown into our tree and bound by fishing line!" We both rejoiced and then prayed to receive the next part of the prayer strategy.

For the next twenty-one days, believers across the state of Kansas and the nation began a period of fasting and prayer in the night hours since Lilith is a nocturnal god. The idea behind this was to pray and war in the night hours when the demonic activity of Lilith is the strongest in order to counter and defeat her diabolical strategies. It was an amazing twenty-one day focus. During this time, new legal cases were instituted against Dr. Tiller and his practice on top of the already existing ones. They focused on his repeated pattern of illegal late-term abortions.

"Tiller now faces two Board of Healing Arts investigations that could cost him his license. He faces 19 criminal counts of illegal late-term abortions that could cost him huge fines, and he faces a grand jury investigation that could net literally hundreds of additional counts of illegal abortions from the past five years that could cost him his freedom," said Operation Rescue President Troy Newman.[9]

Even patients began to come forward and give shocking revelations of all the illegal reasons and actions surrounding their abortions in Tiller's clinic, Women's Health Care Services.[10]

From 2007 on, things continually intensified for Dr. Tiller. He was perpetually involved in court hearings and repeated accounts of his illegal activities within his medical practices were being exposed. And statistics show that the abortion rate of post-viability abortions performed at Tiller's clinic dropped 23 percent in 2007 and the following years. The following is a report from 2009 by Troy Newman, president of Operation Rescue, whose ministry was housed next door to the Tiller clinic:

> During the first part of this year, our focus was on efforts to try late-term abortionist George Tiller for criminal charges that we discovered and exposed. Unfortunately, Tiller was acquitted of performing illegal late-term abortions in March. But minutes after the verdict was read, the Kansas State Board of Healing Arts released a statement indicating that they had filed an 11-count petition against Tiller on those same charges, and that the burden of proof was different than in a criminal case. They assured us that the case was

progressing. Those counts were based on a complaint filed by Operation Rescue staff. We expected to see discipline, perhaps even the revocation of Tiller's license, within six months.[11]

This, obviously, is what we had prayed for, and we felt that the hand of God was working to put a stop to Dr. Tiller's activities.

On May 31, 2009, George Tiller was fatally shot in the foyer of his church. I will state emphatically that in the midst of our praying, not one time did we pray or even consider praying for Tiller's demise. Our hearts' cry was for his spirit to soften and turn from this practice of aborting babies. We prayed for his salvation and God's subsequent blessing on him. The news that he had been gunned down in his home church was appalling, sad, and repulsive to those of us who had been praying. The abortion clinic, of course, was closed and the atrocities he was performing in the murdering of babies in late-term abortion stopped.

Every time I read this, I am overwhelmed. This entire encounter and victorious answer to prayer was so miraculous. And friends, we are living in a time in which Roe v. Wade has been overturned. It is my heart's cry as I am sure it is for many of us that we see abortion overturned and made illegal in every state in our nation. As we close this chapter, let's take time to repent and pray for any areas in our lives where we have aligned with Lilith and all her evil agendas and practices.

Personal Prayer

Father, thank You for Your awesome love and truth. Jesus, thank You for the price You paid on the cross and that through Your blood I am free! Holy Spirit, I welcome You; thank You for Your presence and anointing for deliverance and healing to rest on me from the top of my head to the soles of my feet.

Jesus, I confess that there are areas in my family bloodline and my life that have been influenced and rooted in Lilith structures. I repent for the transgressional cycle I have come in agreement with whether intentional, unknowingly, coerced, or forced. I repent for the sin of partnering with and seeking darkness through practices, beliefs, worship, and the perpetuating of Lilith and her darkness.

I repent for my participation in all forms of ancient or modern Lilith worship and empowerments by way of funding and support of abortion clinics, laws, legislation that empowers eugenics, race suppression, control, aiding in legalizing occult abortions for ritualistic use, all medical abortions, funding or working for organizations within social structures promoting the use of drugs and procedures that aid infertility and eugenics along with diseases and death including other organizations influenced by Lilith, such as secret societies, fraternities, sororities, and all feminist organizations.

I repent for my involvement and participation with Lilith's workings within music festivals like EDM (electronic dance music), psychedelic raves, and Lilith fairs.

I repent for consuming media, gaming, training, and accepting Lilith mystery and knowledge including the ideology of male and female being subservient to sensual acts, divine feminism ideology, the practices of mental and physical meditation and exercises rooted in Lilith.

I repent for the covenants, contracts, the learning of dark arts of cult and occult practices, magic, sex magic, psychic, animal shape-shifting, astral projection, enlightened one, spiritual healers, feminine divination, all dreams that have been welcomed involving a spirit of incubus and succubus, ceremonial and ritualist perverse acts, all occult and demonic rituals from the Hermetic Order of the Golden Dawn, Rosicrucianism and Ordo Templi Orientes, Scientology, and all encounters I have had with Lilith and her cohorts.

Jesus, I now ask You to forgive me for all my participation and involvement with Lilith. I receive your forgiveness and that I am cleansed through Your blood. Thank You for breaking me out of her darkness and bringing me into Your marvelous truth and light.

I now denounce the positions, empowerments, and knowledge gained through Lilith culture and worship. I renounce the agreements and covenants made through rituals and involvements in Jungian personality "switches," use of chakras, writing of her name on palm, use of sigils (image meditation and tracing), trances, hypnotic states, astrology, evoking, invoking, vows and mantras, black magic spells.

I renounce bloodletting, vampirism, draining of psychic energy, seduction of darkness, nightmares, terror, and conjuring of her occult knowledge.

I renounce the spirit of death through abortion. I renounce and break all barrenness in my womb, the financial curse of the funding of abortion, the shadow of death.

I renounce my involvements and empowerments through animal ceremonies and rituals, demonization, and use of shape-shifting to prey on others.

Jesus, in Your name I now break the power of Lilith and all she is known and represents as the dark mother, a patron of abortion, night owl, night hag, queen of the night, mother of demons, winged goddess, goddess of death, goddess of witches, the serpent, night thief, vampirism, psychic vampirism, shape-shifter, death of infants, preying on children and mothers, feminist icon, birther of seduction, devourer of lovers, goddess of moon, torment, all enlightenment, spiritual philosophy, ritual divination, occult sciences, eugenics, black magic, demonic perverse acts including Lilu (masculine), Lilitu (feminine), incubus, succubus, jealousy, passions, whoredom, rage, vengeance, alchemy, along with all powers of darkness off my life and the life of my descendants in Jesus' name!

I declare in Your presence, Jesus, that I am free from these bondages and their effects in my life. Thank You for bringing me into Your light, Your truth, and victorious freedom. Jesus, I now welcome Your healing touch in my body, soul, and spirit that is restoring me to the original purposes that You have destined for me. Holy Spirit, I welcome You to fill me up to overflowing in every area where my house has been swept clean. Father, thank You for Your goodness. Jesus, thank You for redeeming me. Holy Spirit, thank You for Your presence. I ask that You fill me with healing, joy, peace, comfort, the truth of Your word. I welcome more of You in my life. I love You, Lord. Amen.

Research Guidelines for Informed Intercession

Now let's apply this to cities, regions, states, nations, or spheres of influence. As a reminder, these questions serve as a launching pad to advance in the assignments that is He is revealing. During this research process, continue in glory-anointed worship and intercession, welcoming His presence to fill into the city, region, and spheres of influence. Stay in that surrendered place as a prophetic watchman and intercessor standing and believing for revival and awakening. It is also so very key to engage in action steps to ensure a righteous Kingdom voice is being heard concerning abortion and same-sex marriage legislation. Pray and act in letting your voice be heard.

1. Are there Wiccan covens active in your region or sphere of influence?

2. What other forms of the occult are active that engage in Lilith worship?

3. Is there any influence of the Hermetic Order of the Golden Dawn ?

4. Is there an Ordo Templi Orientis occult lodge or group engaging in this form of witchcraft and magic?

5. Is there a strong homosexual, lesbian, transgender community in your region/sphere of influence?

6. Are Wiccan and witchcraft covens actively engaged in local schools? Colleges? Universities?

7. Is there a strong and active presence of the feminist movement in the region/sphere of influence?

8. Have local government or business leaders endorsed and supported the LGBTQ agenda? If so, has identificational repentance occurred?

9. Are there medical practices or universities perpetuating Jungian psychology?

10. Where are the abortion clinics in the region? Is there more than one? Who brought them in?

11. Is there a Planned Parenthood clinic in the region? How many abortions do they perform annually? Do they practice late-term abortion? Medical abortion (the abortion pill)?

12. How has feminism and the occult affected the local government? Who were the first to welcome this into this sphere?

13. How has feminism affected local businesses?

14. Are these groups engaged in the schools and education system?

15. I was not able to teach in-depth about the indigenous history within regions. Usually there is a form

of Lilith worship, but the entity will have a different name. Sometimes she is called the deer woman.

16. What are the prophetic and redemptive promises of the Lord?

17. What are His Kingdom strategies of stewardship of those words?

18. Have there been past moves of revival? If so, pray in agreement that those wells of revival will be awakened again.

19. How is the Lord moving now? Identify those areas and pray in agreement with the moves of His Spirit. Intercede for more of His glorious presence, for revival and awakening.

20. Intercede for revival and awakening in the churches and spheres of culture and influence.

Chapter Six

ISIS

Then God spoke all these words: "I am the Lord your God,
who has brought you out of the land of Egypt, out of the house
of slavery. You shall have no other gods before Me. You shall
not make for yourself any idol, or any likeness (form, mani-
festation) of what is in heaven above or on the earth beneath
or in the water under the earth [as an object to worship]. You
shall not worship them nor serve them; for I, the Lord your
God, am a jealous (impassioned) God [demanding what
is rightfully and uniquely mine], visiting (avenging) the
iniquity (sin, guilt) of the fathers on the children [that is,
calling the children to account for the sins of their fathers], to
the third and fourth generations of those who hate Me, but
showing graciousness and steadfast lovingkindness to thou-
sands [of generations] of those who love Me and keep My
commandments" (Exodus 20:1-6 AMP).

For over 400 years, the children of Israel had lived in a culture
steeped in idolatrous worship that involved evil, dark occult

rituals and ceremonies of black magic, witchcraft, and divination. It was imperative as they were coming out of Egypt that all of the profane and demonic worship of Egypt come out of them. He is the I Am and no other gods are to take His place or rob His worship. While many of us are familiar with these verses, let's study them briefly.

The first commandment (the first sentence above) is directed primarily against the worship of spirits (demons) through spiritism, divination, and idolatry. The second commandment forbids the worship of other gods and any image made of them. It also prohibits making an idol in the image of anything in heaven, meaning the Lord God Himself. The worship of God is not to be directed toward an object; it is based on His Word—His revelation in the Person of Jesus and a personal, intimate relationship with Him.

The actual Hebrew word used in this scripture for sin is *avown*. It is translated "iniquity, guilt, a judicial state of being liable for a wrong done" (Strong's #H5771). If past generations in families have worshipped idols, turned their backs on God, or hated God, it opens a door for strongholds to be passed down the family line. And to expound further, the entire culture of Egypt, meaning every sphere, was engaged in idolatry and occult divination. Our Heavenly Father wanted to ensure personal freedom, and He was also speaking to them as a people and a nation. Nothing of this sort was to be allowed in their worship or spheres of culture as an entire people group and nation in their new day of freedom. How they chose to align their spiritual practices would affect the generations to come. If worship enthroned darkness and evil, it then opened a door of demonic oppression to the third and fourth generation.

The good news is His graciousness, loving-kindness, and mercy extends to a thousand generations for those who obeyed and loved Him. And Jesus as our Savior is forgiving and extends full grace and mercy: "*His mercy extends to those who fear him, from generation to generation*" (Luke 1:50 NIV). Therefore, we can repent of personal sin and the sin that occurred in ancestors in the family line, be set free from its demonic grip, and provide a righteous inheritance for ourselves and the generations to come.

WORSHIP OF ANCIENT EGYPT

What I am about to share will again sound like a storyline and plot played out of a Hollywood movie. But it is the foundational storyline of the demonic entities, demonic worship structure, and belief system that permeated the entire Egyptian culture in the ancient times of the Pharoah. I will say this before going further. I love Egypt and the Egyptian people. It is a nation and a people that the Lord has placed deeply in my heart.

We have extensively researched and spiritually mapped the history of Egypt. In this process, we have been to numerous sites where we learned through archeologists and historians. It is necessary to share because the deities worshipped and the practices surrounding them are the origins of all Masonic beliefs and every branch of this secret order: Blue Lodge, Scottish Rite, York Rite, Shriners, Order of the Eastern Star, Daughters of Isis, DeMolay, Job's Daughters, and all college fraternities and sororities just to name a few. There is not a nation in which Masonry has not touched or established itself, building its ideologies within the fabric of that culture. And the spiritual practices of the nation, including all worship to false gods and goddesses, has syncretized into Freemasonry. As many are aware, Freemasonry is firmly established in the United States.

As the tale of the ancient demonic principalities is revealed, throughout the storyline I will bring in some of the aspects of its active role in Masonry. For the sake of space and to keep focused, we will keep our emphasis on the main characters/deities shared below. But I will state this: there are some Christians who are members of the Masonic Order, which means they have partnered with all of the false demonic worship beliefs and practices in Freemasonry. Christians should have no place or involvement in this occult order.

RA, OSIRIS, ISIS, HORUS

Ra was the leading god of Egypt known as the sun god. It was believed that he was self-created. In the ancient Egyptian creation story, Ra stood on the primordial mound among swirling waters of chaos and established order from chaos, created other gods, and spoke the world into existence. Order out of chaos is the stated purpose for the highest Masonic initiation and honor, the 33rd degree.

Ra was the father of Osiris, Isis, Nephthys, and Set. The name *Osiris* means powerful and the seeing eye. *Isis* means *throne* or *seated*. Her identity was the moon goddess and mother of all. *Nephthys* means mistress of the mansion, and *Set* represents chaos and confusion.

Weary of humanity and his role as the supreme ruler, Ra handed his reign to Osiris, who married his sister Isis, while Set, jealous and plotting, married the other sister, Nephthys. As is evident, this tale introduces themes of perversion through incest. Trust me, in my years of experience in deliverance ministry and praying strategically for regions, perversion is a stronghold in Masonry.

Osiris, before being enthroned, embarked on a journey to explore Egypt's welfare and agriculture. He was unaware of Set's jealous, evil, and fatal plot against him, which involved a custom sarcophagus (Egyptian coffin). You see, in ancient Egypt they prepared their entire life for death. The more wealth attained in life and taken into the burial chamber, the higher the status as a god in the afterlife.

Set crafted a sarcophagus from acacia wood and gold, symbolizing extravagant wealth and ensuring divine status in the afterlife. This act mirrors satan's counterfeit and darker intentions, as the materials match those of the Ark of the Covenant, highlighting his evil mockery of what is holy to our Heavenly Father.

Set hosted a celebration and feast for Osiris's return, introducing a game to see who fit into the ornately crafted sarcophagus for a burial prize. Others tried but didn't fit; Osiris did, falling into Set's trap. The lid was sealed with molten material; Osiris was entombed alive and set adrift in the Nile. He soon died inside the sarcophagus, drifted down the Nile into the Mediterranean Sea, and came aground in ancient Biblos, which is modern-day Lebanon. This event mirrors Masonic rites where initiates symbolically are lowered into a coffin depicting their death and then raised up into the resurrection of Osiris.

Having heard of Osiris' fate, Isis and her sister Nephthys embarked on a quest to recover his body, locating it in the temple of the King of Biblos. Who, having discovered the sarcophagus on land with an acacia tree growing from it, perceived it as a divine sign and placed it in the temple for worship.

After finding Osiris, Isis and Nephthys began their return to Egypt. Along the way they stopped to rest in a cave. There, Isis used an ankh, the ancient witchcraft symbol of resurrection life, to raise Osiris from the dead. She performed this magic by breathing her breath of life through the ankh into his body. Again, a mockery and counterfeit of satan as our Heavenly Father is the one who breathed His breath of life into Adam so that he became a living soul (Genesis 2:7). Isis and Osiris were overjoyed, which led to a moment of passion in which Horus was conceived. Exhausted by this whole ordeal, Osiris fell into a deep sleep. Isis left the cave. In Masonry, the infamous symbol of the point within the circle represents this erotic moment and union between Isis and Osiris.

Envious Set, upon hearing about the rescue and resurrection plan, sought to kill Osiris again. He found him asleep in the cave, dismembered him into fourteen pieces, and dispersed them across Egypt. Set cast Osiris' manhood into the river where some myths state it was eaten by a crocodile with others state it remained in the Nile enhancing its fertility.

Masonry employs its own version of prophetic art called tracing boards. Symbolic in nature, these visuals often feature a ladder with fourteen rungs reaching toward the sun, Osiris, or moon, Isis. The fourteen rungs represent the dismembered body parts of Osiris. In the ascension to the top of the ladder there is great enlightenment. Thus, the initiate becomes like Osiris.

Isis and Nephthys returned to the cave to the discovery of Set's fatal assault against Osiris. They embarked again on a journey, gathering all fourteen body parts. Isis put the dismembered pieces of Osiris' body together. She realized his manhood was missing and fashioned him a new phallus from the dirt of the land. Once more, she breathed her breath of life though the ankh into Osiris. Again, he was resurrected. Due to his previous castration he was infertile, which caused his status and title to change to the god of the underworld.

Upon Horus' birth, he was hailed as the savior and the omniscient one, symbolized by the Eye of Horus within a triangle, representing the all-seeing eye. This symbol was added to the dollar bill on Vice President Henry Wallace's recommendation during Franklin Roosevelt's presidency. Wallace was a Mason, an occultist, and member of the Theosophical Society founded by Madame Helena P. Blavatsky, who will be further discussed.

Set was the next in the inherited line of Ra's sons to take the throne. He was rejected by the Egyptians as a ruler due to his evil actions, jealousy, and rebellion. Therefore, they constructed obelisks in all fourteen locations where the dismembered pieces of Osiris' body had been sent, the top of each being capped with gold.

Some might be inquiring about the significance and meaning of the obelisk. "It is four-sided free-standing pillar...tapering inward as it rises, terminating in a small pyramid. They were apparently seen as resembling the rays of the sun, the podium being the primeval hill over which the sun rose and became symbolic of royal rejuvenation. Jer. 43:13 refers to the obelisks of Heliopolis, literally "the pillars of the sun temple which is in Egypt."[1] To put it plainly, an obelisk represents the phallus of Osiris. The gold capped apex, triangle, at the top signifies Horus. It is a universal Masonic symbol and structure.

At sunrise, as the sun ascended over the top of the obelisks capped with gold, rays of light would shoot out across the land of Egypt. It was believed that Osiris was having relations with himself to regenerate the world and the heavens. In the evening, as the moon ascended the top of the obelisk, it represented Isis, the moon goddess, having relations with Osiris, with the gold capped triangle representing the conception of Horus—the promised child and savior, the all-seeing and all-knowing child god of Egypt, the heavens and the earth.

What an unpleasant story and belief system! But it is the true spiritual belief and worship of ancient Egypt. It is what Moses lived in while growing up in Pharoah's household and what the Israelites were enslaved in. A culture steeped in idolatrous worship that involved white magic and black magic. And as previously stated, sadly, this is the spiritual foundational belief of the secret society of Freemasons and all of its branches and divisions.

Some will be aware, but, yes, the Washington Monument in Washington D.C. is an obelisk that was funded and built by Masons. Within the walls of the monument are twenty-two masonic stones, "14 from Grand Lodges, and 8 from individual Lodges."[2]

At noon on July 4, 1848, the Grand Master of Masons of the District of Columbia, Benjamin Brown French, led the cornerstone laying ceremony in the presence of President Polk and numerous dignitaries. Grand Master French began the ceremony…"I now present to you, my Brother, the square, level, and plumb, which are the working tools you are to use in the erection of this monument. You, as a Freemason, know to what they morally allude…Look well to the erection of this National Monument; see that every stone is well squared, and that it is placed in its position both level and plumb, so that this noble offering of a nation to commemorate greatness, patriotism, and virtue, may stand until the end of time."[3]

Truth be told, the majority of the architecture and mapping out of our nation's capital, along with many capital cities throughout the United States, were designed and laid out by Masonic architects in honor of Osiris, Isis, Horus, and the Great Architect of the Universe.

The universal symbol of Masons is the triangle and compass containing the letter G in the center. It is an occult symbol to the ancient Egyptian deities. As is stated by Albert Pike, the renowned Master Mason who also served on the Supreme Council of the Southern Jurisdiction:

The Hermaphroditic figure is the Symbol of the double nature anciently assigned to the Deity, as Generator and Producer, as…Osiris and Isis among the Egyptians. As the Sun was male, so the Moon was female; and Isis was both the sister and the wife of Osiris. The Compass, therefore, is the Hermetic Symbol of the Creative Deity, and the Square of the productive Earth or Universe.[4]

The "G" in the center of the compass and square stands for the Great Architect of the Universe.

The phrase "Grand Architect" appears in Masonic rituals in various forms, such as "Grand Geometrician of the Universe"... "Great Geometrician".... The word "Geometry" here refers to "sacred geometry", which is a system of measuring and constructing the world and cosmos that was first developed by the Ancient Egyptians and Greeks but has been used by many cultures throughout history.[5]

Further, according to Masonic teaching the "G" refers to or represents the God or deity of any world religion. It simultaneously represents the God of the Bible, Allah, Buddha, Confucius, Zoroaster, satan, or whatever god the initiate into Masonry personally worships.

As shared in this lore of ancient Egypt, Isis was the demonic entity that had the power of resurrection life. Therefore, in ancient Egypt she was considered the holiest of all and the mother of all.

"I am," says Isis, "Nature; parent of all things, the sovereign of the Elements, the primitive progeny of Time, the most exalted of the Deities, the first of the Heavenly

Gods and Goddesses, the Queen of the Shades, the uniform countenance; who dispose with my rod the numerous lights of Heaven, the salubrious breezes of the sea, and the mournful silence of the dead; whose single Divinity the whole world venerates in many forms, with various rites and by many names. The Egyptians…call me by my true name, Isis the Queen."[6]

Albert Pike also echoes her words:

I am Isis, Queen of this country. I was instructed by Mercury. No one can destroy the laws which I have established. I am the eldest daughter of Saturn, most ancient of the Gods.[7]

For many the masonic architecture of our nation's capital and many of the capital cities within our nation is not new revelation. The great news is there has been effective and victorious break-through prayer that has occurred concerning the architectural layout of Washington D.C. and many cities. As shared in the following testimony by my friends Jon and Jolene Hamill:

On July 4, 2011, Jolene and I hosted apostle John Benefiel and a gathering of apostolic leaders…at the Lincoln Memorial.

On the anniversary of the signing of the Declaration of Independence, we presented the project the Lord had mandated we fulfill. A petition called the Declaration of Covenant, seeking the reconstitution of the covenant our forefathers had made. I was privileged to write this proposal, seeking God's hand in marriage to our land once again.

We boldly asked for a sign that God had approved this covenant restoration. Prophet Rick Ridings had seen a vision of a nutcracker which cracked a hard shell of demonic resistance over Washington DC. Our request was framed accordingly, "Lord, grant the fullness of this divorcement from Baal. Grant a restoration of covenant with You. And as a sign that You have heard us, crack the hard shell of resistance!"

Fifty days later to the day, our request was answered. On August 23, an unprecedented earthquake measuring 5.8 on the Richter scale shook Washington DC. Gargoyles toppled from the National Cathedral. The altar of a prominent temple to Baal was damaged. Even the Washington Monument cracked in the earthquake![8]

Woohoo! Come on God! As previously stated, there is not one country or cultural sphere of influence that Freemasonry has not impacted. Osiris, Isis, Horus—the demonic trinity is still prevalent in the nations of the world through the secret societies of Freemasonry, Rosicrucian, Shriners, Scottish Rite, York Rite, Knights Templar, and many others. Truthfully, this chapter could be an entire book mapping out how Isis, Osiris, and Horus have impacted culture. With that being said, let's continue to gain understanding of how these entities continue to exert a demonic grip within modern culture. Keep in mind this is a brief description. Each of you reading will also need to look into your area and spheres of influence for further research. It is the Lord's desire and plan that all of us have testimonies of victory!

ORDER OF THE EASTERN STAR

The organization known as the Eastern Star is intended for the mothers, wives, sisters, and daughters of Freemasons. Established in 1850 by Freemason Robert Morris, it operates with a ritual structure affiliated to that of the men's lodge but utilizing only five degrees. Central to its symbolism is an inverted pentagram, which to some evokes associations with satan, dark magic, and rebellion against religious norms. Additionally, it finds usage in various New Age, Wiccan, and occult practices. Within the Eastern Star and broader Masonic traditions, there is a profound emphasis on the symbol of the point within a circle as referenced by my friend Selwyn Stevens in his book Signs and Symbols.

> Masonic literature states "this union of the phallus and the cteis, which is well represented by the point within a circle, was intended by the ancients as a type of the prolific powers of nature, which they worshipped under the united form of the active or male principle, and the passive or female principle."[9]

DAUGHTERS OF ISIS

Daughters of Isis, also known as the Imperial Court of Daughters, is an auxiliary branch of female family members of Prince Hall Shriners. It was initially organized at the annual session of the Ancient Egyptian Arabic Order Noble Mystic Shrine held in Detroit, Michigan, on August 24, 1910. Their stated purpose is to unite the relatives of all members of both branches into one common bond of friendship, to practice charity and to instill honor and integrity, as symbolized in the legend of the Egyptian Queen, the Goddess Isis. The following gives insight to their initiation:

> Instead of being the usual milk-and-water Christian-ized version of a male ritual. The oath in which the postulant agrees to a penalty of having her body sliced in 14 parts and thrown into a river is also unusual in a women's organization. There is still the normal religious aspects of ritual which the candidate kisses the Bible three times, Al-Quran once, and a red stone.[10]

RESURGENCE OF OCCULTISM IN THE 19TH CENTURY

The 19th century was known as the time of the occult revival. A central figure was Helena P. Blavatsky also referred to as H.P.B. In 1874, she met General Henry Steel Olcott, an American military officer, lawyer, and Mason. Both were fascinated with the occult. Together, they formed the Theosophical Society in New York City in 1875. It is considered a key movement in the development of modern occultism. Blavatsky's teachings, as well as those of subsequent leaders, had a profound impact on various occult and esoteric traditions that emerged in the late 19th and early 20th centuries.

To give a brief history, she was born in Russia. Her grandfather was a Mason. She spent much of her time as a young girl reading his Masonic books, which greatly influenced the spiritual path that she embarked on in the occult. Family members said she had psychic and clairvoyant abilities from a young age and would often refer to having seen her master (meaning an adept or occult spiritualist) from Tibet in her dreams.

In 1851, she met this master in Hyde Park while he was traveling with a contingent of princes from India. He told her of her subsequent training and calling to be an adept—one who has gained knowledge of alchemy (hidden mysteries and knowledge), the occult, mystical philosophy, and magic. Those who knew her personally tell that she spent three and possibly up to seven years in Tibet training with this master, Morya, in the occult, Buddhism, and Hinduism.

She also spent three years in Egypt, 1871–1873, where she engaged in a variety of esoteric and mystical activities, occultism, and spiritualism. The focus was the pursuit of spiritual enlightenment and discovery of hidden knowledge through spiritual initiation into Egyptian mysteries. These initiations involved meditation, channeling of demonic entities, and awakening to an ability to function as a medium. Throughout her life, she led many séances.

The Theosophical Society promoted the study of comparative religion, philosophy, and science, and it explored spiritual and metaphysical concepts from around the world. Blavatsky's major works, such as *The Secret Doctrine* and *Isis Unveiled*, introduced Western audiences to Eastern religions including Hinduism, Buddhism, and Tibetan Buddhism. While writing *Isis Unveiled*, she described her spiritual experience in a letter to her sister Vera:

> Well Vera, whether you believe me or not, something extraordinary is happening to me, you cannot imagine in what a charmed world of pictures and visions I live. I'm writing Isis, not writing, but rather copying out and drawing that which she personally shows to me. Upon

my word sometimes it seems to me that the ancient goddess of beauty in person leads me through all the countries of past centuries which I have to describe.[11]

INFLUENCE IN MODERN SPIRITUALITY

In the realm of modern spirituality, the legacy of Isis has a profound demonic impact. As discussed in Chapter Four, the Hermetic Order of the Golden Dawn founded in the late 19th century has continued to exert influence into the 20th century. Within its rituals it synthesized western occult mysticism including kabbalah, hermeticism, alchemy, and Egyptian mythology. In the Golden Dawn system, Isis plays a significant role in their demonic rituals symbolizing rebirth, magic, and the mysteries of the divine feminine.

This syncretism of the Golden Dawn and the occult teachings of Madame Blavatsky became the demonic open door to contemporary pagan and neo-pagan movements such as Wicca, the Fellowship of Isis, the new age movement, and many others. Within the deception of these sects she is also revered as a caring mother who brings healing, protection, and awakens mastery over magic and the afterlife. Practitioners often look to Isis for guidance in rituals and spells, drawing upon her wisdom and strength to navigate life's challenges through invoking and activating their divine femininity through a relationship with her. Friends, this is complete demonic witchcraft and magic.

To her initiates, the goddess's attributes of rebirth and renewal make her particularly significant representing the cyclic nature of life and the possibility of transformation. One of the ways this is achieved is through empowering kundalini. This definitely exhibits the syncretism of occult beliefs between Egypt and India. Kundalini comes from Hinduism in the ancient history of India. It is a coiled serpent demonic spirit that wraps itself around the base of the spine, traveling upwards through all of the energy channels of the body known as chakras. Those who engage in this demonic empowerment claim that it causes spiritual enlightenment and expansion of consciousness. The truth is this is a dark demonic spirit that will overtake a life and eventually cause serious infirmity and death. Many who practice yoga, occult meditation, and pranayama (occult breath control), whether knowing or unknowingly have given a red-carpet invitation to a kundalini spirit.

FEMINISM AND GENDER EDUCATION

Theosophy, like other occult and esoteric movements, was particularly attractive to feminists drawn to the occult. Blavatsky's influential works, *Isis Unveiled* and *The Secret Doctrine,* were pivotal in shaping feminist discussion on ancient and contemporary goddesses. Her writings provided a foundation for occult feminists to challenge patriarchal norms, offering narratives that empowered women. Within the Theosophical Society, female members found significance and a new voice. *The Secret Doctrine* reshaped gender relations. As a result, Isis became a central archetype for many in feminist movements.

Dion Fortune is noted as a strong voice who pioneered the contemporary image of Isis as the woman, in her book *All Women Are Isis.* There are also two other women who were influential members of the Theosophical Society in this occult-driven feminism movement: Frances Swiney (1847–1922), a writer and women's suffrage activist and spokesperson; Florence Farr (1860–1917), a British actress and writer. Both were also members of the Fabian Society, the Eugenics Educational Society. The Fabian Society is a British socialist organization founded in 1884 with the vision of advancing socialist principles through gradual means of reform. Both women had significant voices within feminism, locally and internationally, advancing the beliefs of Isis. For the sake of space, I will not belabor their entire stories but will briefly share their impact.

Frances Swiney wrote eight books and numerous articles and publications. She combined Theosophical theories of matriarchal ancient religions and identified Isis to be the mother of all. In 1909, from her education of Isis within the Theosophical Society, she was inspired to launch her own society, the League of Isis. It soon established lodges in South Africa, India, and the US. Its objective was to educate youth on sexual diseases as well as the Law of Isis, also referred to as the Law of the Mother.

Florence Farr was a true devotee of Isis. I find it interesting that she was also a member of the Hermetic Order of the Golden Dawn. In 1892, Isis appeared to her in a vision describing herself as the Mother of All, origin of the world, the most powerful existing force.[12] She also recalls another vision, where Isis spoke the following:

> I am the mother Mother Isis; most powerful of all the
> world, I am she who fights not but is always victorious,
> I am that Sleeping Beauty whom men have sought, for

all time…I am lifted up on high, and do draw men onto me. Love is the Mother of Man.[13]

As a result of her veneration of Isis and complete engagement as a feminist occult voice, in 1897 Farr became the initiated leader of the British Isis-Urania Temple, the first lodge of the Hermetic Order of the Golden Dawn. She did so under the direct commissioning of one the three founders, Samuel Liddell MacGregor Mathers.

VICTORY AT THE GATE

We have taken this historical and mapping journey of this principality through ancient history to a few samplings of its modern-day manifestation. I would like to share a testimony in which breakthrough occurred at an ancient Isis gate.

Alice Smith led a team to Egypt in 1995. I was invited and served as her co-leader. I was young! Twenty-eight years old! As we researched in preparation for the assignment, we discovered that we would be dealing with ancient roots of Freemasonry. One of the team members, whom I will call "Paul," had been a 33rd degree Mason, as had his father before him. When Paul discovered the truth about Freemasonry, he denounced his connection with it, broke all ties with it, and threw out anything he owned that was related to it. The Lord told us that Paul would be the point man of the trip and would be used powerfully.

We scheduled a day to visit the ruins of a temple located in ancient Tanis, the region we would know from the Bible as Goshen. The biblically historic region of Egypt that Joseph,

Jacob, Moses, the Children of Israel, Joshua, and Jeremiah all resided in. It was greatly built up and fortified by King Shishak and his twenty-second dynasty of rulers. We believed him to be one of the initiators of what we would now term Masonic practices of occult veneration and rituals to Osiris, Isis, Horus, and Ra. Shishak is mentioned in the Bible:

> *In the fifth year of King Rehoboam, Shishak king of Egypt attacked Jerusalem. He carried off the treasures of the temple of the Lord and the treasures of the royal palace. He took everything, including all the gold shields Solomon had made* (1 Kings 14:25-26 NIV).

No doubt this brought a curse to this region and to Egypt.

Paul was in intercession all night and all day before we arrived at this location. It seemed evident that something strategic was about to occur. When we arrived, we learned that the site was closed because of excavations. Gigi, our guide, was a Christian on fire for God. She got out of the van to convince the workers to let us in. I must pause and mention a bit of background information. Because I have the same skin and hair coloring of Egyptian women, many people thought I was Egyptian. (On this trip, I actually received three marriage proposals; one man offered Alice a thousand camels for me!) Well, at this location my "new identity" came in handy. We could see that Gigi was having a difficult time. Alice instructed me to sit in the front seat of the van, take off my sunglasses, and smile at the men overseeing the entrance to the site. It worked! We hid our amusement as they ushered us in.

When we entered the ruins we were astonished. All around us stood large obelisks, and on each of these obelisks were hieroglyphics depicting Isis, Osiris, Horus, Ra. These hieroglyphics also included the Masonic symbols that we still see today. We went to the entrance gate of the temple to pray. Gigi told us to pray quickly because she was not going to be able to stall the workers much longer.

Paul prayed prayers of identificational repentance and denounced Freemasonry as a demonic secret society. Alice instructed him to break the power of Freemasonry—Ra, Osiris, Isis, Horus—off the land and to cut its power to all the nations where it had spread. As soon as Paul made this authoritative declaration, it instantly began to rain. We were excited, undone, and began to weep.

Gigi instructed us to leave quickly because the workers were losing patience. We promptly obliged. Once in the van she asked, "Do you understand the miracle we are in?" We replied, "Yes, the Lord told us He would come in the clouds, rain, and He did." Gigi then told us, "I am thirty-three years old; I was born and raised in Egypt. This is the month of October, which is considered the dry season. I have never in my life seen it rain in Egypt in the dry season. This has never happened." We were all floored!

Friends, it rained a lot! It was a Houston, Texas, kind of rain. It lasted four hours with strong gusty winds. That night at dinner, the hotel and restaurant staff were standing at the windows watching it rain. They did not know what to think. As we left the restaurant that evening, the manager was standing by the door watching it rain. We asked what he thought about it. His answer proved to us that God can use anyone to confirm His plans. This man did not know who we were and had not met us, but he looked right at us and responded, "It is because you are here that it rained." Speechless, all six of us turned the corner to leave the restaurant and immediately began to weep.

The final amount of the rainfall was one and three-fourths inches. The normal annual rainfall in that part of the world is one inch. God can and will manifest in the natural realm breakthrough that has occurred in the spiritual realm. He is an awesome and miraculous God!

The most exciting and confirming news is I was able to return to Egypt recently. It had been twenty-eight years since the strategic prayer journey. Everyone still talks about the history-making rainfall of 1995. All the Christian leaders we met still speak of that moment as a sign and wonder from heaven of victory and breakthrough.

JESUS SITS ON THE THRONE!

I don't know about all who are reading, but I am ready to declare and see His truth exalted above all and every demonic scheme of this goddess Isis and these demonic entities that have deceived and trapped so many in the Theosophical Society, feminism, occult, witchcraft, and all forms of Freemasonry. Let's stop and declare the following scripture out loud!

> *And [I pray] that the eyes of your heart [the very center and core of your being] may be enlightened [flooded with light by the Holy Spirit], so that you will know and*

cherish the hope [the divine guarantee, the confident expectation] to which He has called you, the riches of His glorious inheritance in the saints (God's people), and [so that you will begin to know] what the immeasurable and unlimited and surpassing greatness of His [active, spiritual] power is in us who believe. These are in accordance with the working of His mighty strength which He produced in Christ when He raised Him from the dead and seated Him at His own right hand in the heavenly places, far above all rule and authority and power and dominion [whether angelic or human], and [far above] every name that is named [above every title that can be conferred], not only in this age and world but also in the one to come (Ephesians 1:18-21 AMP).

Personal Prayer

Father, thank You for Your amazing love. Jesus, thank You that through Your truth and by Your blood I am healed and set free. Holy Spirit, I welcome You to come now with Your anointing for healing and deliverance. Jesus, I confess all involvement with Isis and her many manifestations. I confess all cultural, social, and Masonic influence within my family's bloodline. I repent for my own sin and transgressions where I came into agreement and made a covenant known or unknown to Isis, welcoming her into my soul to gain power. I repent for glorifying her through seeking mysteries and hidden knowledge and invoking her power.

I repent for spiritual hypnotic states, meditation, releasing of occult sounds in music, all perverse acts, infliction of pain, bloodletting, and ceremonies with fire.

I repent for all practices of occultic breathing rituals: yoga, reiki (seeking out dark or light feminine energies), kundalini empowerment, divine feminism, ceremonies engaging in rebirth of death to life.

I repent for inviting dream visitations, all occultic forms of transformation (physical, mental, psychic), mixing of concoctions and tonics for healing, spiritual guides/enlightenment in this life or afterlife, in death and spiritualist healings.

I repent for establishing altars and ceremonies aligned with equinoxes, feast day celebrations of the moon and sun, solstices, psychic readings, tarot cards, mysticism, spells, use of amulets, counsel of the dead, black stones, mind control, astral projection, magic (black and white).

I repent for ceremonies in businesses and other areas of control for wealth, knowledge, marketing, prosperity. I repent for occult rituals and spells done to control law. I repent for all activities and involvement with every branch of Freemasonry and the using of witchcraft, divination, and secrecy to control government and the way in which people are governed.

I renounce all forms and operations influenced and founded in Isis worship and her false covering in the areas of ancient and modern spiritual divination, including magic (black and white), Wicca, new age, rebirths, mysticism, hermeticism, esoteric movements, the sciences (including medical, mental, alchemy, eugenics, gender transitions), astrology, magic, feminism and divine feminism, education involving occult syncretism, music, self-healing, revealed mysteries, secret societies, cults, covens, and healing practitioners. I break the powers and entanglements of worship to Isis as mother and resurrector of all life, the eldest star, water goddess, earth goddess, and star goddess, the one who receives petitions and releases wisdom, hidden knowledge of witchcraft, secret knowledge, mysteries of all realms, all seeing, life giver-nurturer-producer, breath of life, all self-worship and every name and personification of her from every culture and time. I break you, Isis, off of my finances and all business deals that have been bound by your systems and structures. These are now severed from my life and the life of my descendants in Jesus' name!

I thank You, Jesus, that You are the true creator of life. Your breath is life. Thank You for the gift of salvation. Thank You, Jesus, that You overcame all death, darkness, powers, authorities, the visible and invisible, all things in the heavens and earth—Your blood seals me in Your peace!

Jesus, You are all wisdom and I rejoice and declare that I now have access to wisdom, knowledge, and understanding through Your Word that's alive in me. Thank

You that You heal my diseases and restore my soul from pain, afflictions, and darkness.

Holy Spirit, I welcome You to fill me up to overflowing with life, joy, peace, healing, comfort. Your light guides, directs, and causes my feet to walk good pathways that lead me to wholeness. I speak that I now walk abundantly in health, wealth, and the fruit and gifts of You, Holy Spirit! I am covered in Your robe of righteousness, surrounded and covered in Your glory! I declare that I am free indeed!

Research Guidelines for Informed Intercession

It's time to dig deeper with research guidelines for the assignments He is revealing. Remember in the research process to stay in a place of glory-anointed intercession and the faithful study of His Word. Allow Holy Spirit to guide the spiritual mapping process. Stand in intercession for those who are trapped in darkness to have glorious, life-transforming encounters with Jesus so that they will enter into His marvelous light of redemption and victorious freedom and awakening.

1. Who were the foundational leaders? Were they Masons? Engaged in Eastern Star?
   a. Locate the Masonic and Eastern Star lodges in the region including Prince Hall and Daughters of Isis.
   b. Research government buildings and churches dedicated with a Masonic Cornerstone.
   c. Is there a strong representation of Freemasonry within the spheres of influence?

2. Are there witchcraft covens in operation? Ones that invoke Isis?

3. What other forms of witchcraft and the occult are in operation?

4. Is there an influence of the Theosophical Society?

5. Is there an occult movement of feminism, a strong representation of feminism that is aggressive and manipulative? If so, what spheres of society and culture has this movement impacted?

6. Does it have influence in the sphere of education?

7. Have there been past moves of revival? If so, pray in agreement that those wells of revival will be awakened again.

8. How is the Lord moving now? Identify those areas and pray in agreement with the moves of His Spirit. Intercede for more of His glorious presence, for revival and awakening.

9. Intercede for revival and awakening in the churches and spheres of culture and influence.

10. What are the prophetic and redemptive promises of the Lord?

11. What are His Kingdom strategies of stewardship of those words?

Chapter Seven

JEZEBEL

Jezebel is the wicked woman from the Word of God we have all grown to dislike. Why? Because this spirit is very alive and active in our culture. The meaning of her name is, "where is the prince?" or also "un-husbanded." Isn't it interesting that even the meaning of her name depicts the truly demonic lack of reverence for the Prince of Peace and our Heavenly Father who is a covenant-keeping God. Jezebel, or the one un-husbanded, will always aggressively attack covenants made in righteousness. Her name was actually the ritual cry in the worship of Baal.

Jezebel's story is told in the Books of Kings. She was a Phoenician princess, the daughter of Ethbaal, king of Tyre. First Kings 16:31 says she was "Sidonian," from Zidon, which is generally a biblical term for Phoenicians. In this city and culture of her upbringing and royal influence, the Queen of Heaven was the eminent and supreme ruler. "Ethbaal, also called Ithobalus… was a priest of Astarte, and, having put the king, Pheles, to death, assumed the scepter of Tyre and Sidon, lived sixty-eight years, and reigned thirty-two."[1] We see here the reason Jezebel, the daughter of a priest of Astarte, was so zealous in her promotion of idolatry.

Jezebel married King Ahab of the Northern Kingdom of Israel. He was the son of King Omri, who had brought the northern Kingdom of Israel to great power and established Samaria as his capital. This marriage was the culmination of the friendly relations existing between Israel and Phoenicia during Omri's reign, and possibly cemented important political designs. This was the first time that a king of Israel had allied himself by marriage with a heathen princess; and the alliance was, in this case, disastrous. Let's discuss the two demonic entities that Jezebel in essence sold her soul to.

BAAL

Jezebel, like the foreign wives of Solomon, required facilities and temples for carrying on her forms of worship. Therefore, Ahab made an altar for Baal in the house of Baal, which he had built in Samaria employing 450 prophets in the worship of this principality. He was the supreme male divinity of the Phoenician and Canaanite nations, also known as the sun god. Baal worship is ancient. This practice prevailed in the time of Moses through the Moabites and Midianites. Unfortunately, it spread to the Israelites. Sadly, in the time of the kings it became the religion of the court and people of the ten tribes. Temples were erected to Baal in Judah where he was worshipped with great ceremony. The worship to this principality was wicked and lustful in nature and in many forms, sacrifice and child sacrifice were required. Other names for Baal are Bel, Molech, Marduk, Chemosh.

He was the chief god of the pantheon and celebrated in the spring of the year to venerate the awakening and conception of nature. The medieval Druids, who saw his name as meaning "the shining one," adopted his worship. In his demonic belief, he earned his ranking position in the Babylon pantheon by killing the goddess of chaos, Tiamet (Isaiah 46:1; Jeremiah 50:2 and 51:44). By studying the Word of God we learn that he was worshipped under different adaptations and manifestations according to people, cities, and regions.

1. Baal-Berith: the covenant Baal
2. Baal-Zebub: lord of the fly
3. Baal-Hanan: the name of the early kings of Edom
4. Baal-Peor: lord of the opening
5. Baalath-Beer: lord of the well
6. Baal-Gad: lord of fortune
7. Baal-Hamon: lord of the multitude
8. Baal-Hazor: village of Baal
9. Mount Baal-Hermon: lord of Hermon
10. Baal-Zephon: lord of the hidden things, north and darkness

This ancient principality has also fortified strongholds throughout the nations. But that is another book! Other sun god names are Ra, Osiris, Horus, Apollo, Zeus, Hercules, Nike, Helios, Dazhbog, Sunna, Mithras, Shamash.

ASHERAH

To further meet Jezebel's demands, Ahab also built the cultic symbol of worship to the goddess Asherah. Most scholars and archaeologists agree temples or idols to her were also erected. The cult of Asherah is ancient. In a Sumerian inscription, she is known as the bride of Anu (heaven). In Ugaritic literature she is called Lady Asherah of the sea, a title signifying that she was one who treads on the sea.

Tyre was a major center for her veneration as she was the chief goddess of the region. Here she was revered as consort or wife of El, and the mother of seventy gods, including Baal. Animal sacrifices were offered to her; sexual perversion including temple prostitution with homosexuality were very prevalent. She also bore the title "Holiness" as attested by an Egyptian nude figure of her bearing that inscription.

Her name is frequently translated as groves and her worship, rituals, and ceremonies would frequently occur in groves of trees. The object of her veneration was also called an *Asherah* meaning a sacred pillar. These Asherah poles were erected at sacred sites and alongside altars throughout the land of Canaan "*on every high hill and under every green tree*" (1 Kings 14:23, ESV). The Baal temple at Samaria had an Asherah pole.

> In ancient times these altars were typically built under green trees. The city of Tyre on the Mediterranean coast was home to the best cedars of Lebanon and seemed to have been an important center for the worship of Asherah.[2]

Asherah worship was deeply sensual, involving illicit acts of perversion and ritual prostitution. It was closely associated with the worship of Baal: *"The Israelites did evil in the Lord's sight. They forgot about the Lord their God, and they served the images of Baal and the Asherah poles"* (Judges 3:7 NLT). "At times, to appease Baal and Asherah, human sacrifices were made. These sacrifices usually consisted of the firstborn child of the person making the sacrifice,"[3] as stated in Jeremiah 19:5 (NASB):

> *And have built the high places of Baal to burn their sons in the fire as burnt offerings to Baal, a thing which I never commanded or spoke of, nor did it ever enter My mind.*

All idol and demonic worship and veneration was explicitly forbidden by the Lord: *"You must never set up a wooden Asherah pole beside the altar you build for the Lord your God"* (Deuteronomy 16:21 NLT). When Asa reigned in Judah:

> *He banished the male and female shrine prostitutes from the land and got rid of all the idols his ancestors had made. He even deposed his grandmother Maacah from her position as queen mother because she had made an obscene Asherah pole. He cut down her obscene pole and burned it in the Kidron Valley* (1 Kings 15:12-13 NLT).

Jezebel highly venerated Asherah and ensured her worship by commissioning four hundred prophets.[4] These prophets were welcomed to have a close relationship with Jezebel as they ate at her table, which would involve eating a meal, but also an invitation into the bedroom for licentious encounters. Jezebel stamped her name on history as the representative of all that is designing, crafty, malicious, revengeful, and cruel believing she was the human manifestation and personification of the Queen of Heaven. Jezebel went so far as to require that her religion should be the national religion of Israel. After all, in her culture, the Queen of Heaven was ruler of all.

JEZEBEL KILLED PROPHETS

We see in scripture that Jezebel also killed prophets of Israel: *"When Jezebel killed the prophets of the Lord, Obadiah took a hundred prophets and hid them in groups of fifty in a cave and fed them with bread and water"* (1 Kings 18:4 MEV), positioning her as the first great instigator of persecution against the children of Israel. She was guided by no principle, restrained by no fear of either God or man, passionate in her attachment to her heathen worship; she spared no limits to maintain idolatry around her in all its demonic splendor. The idolatry, as we have discussed, was of the most debased and sensual kind in which their rituals involved depraved and licentious practices and abominations. Human sacrifice, sometimes child sacrifice, was often made to appease Jezebel's pagan desires.

You see, when the sun god Baal, lord of all, and the moon goddess Asherah, queen of all, are given the place of rulership by those in authority, the prophets and prophetic voice will be silenced or killed. Why? They zealously opposed all that Jezebel and Ahab believed and were perpetuating. The prophets posed a threat to Jezebel's religious or, better stated, diabolical spiritual agenda. Their rule faced opposition from these prophets, who spoke out against their policies, particularly those that promoted idolatry, human sacrifice, and injustice. The prophets were seen as threats to her and her husband's authority; therefore, she sought to suppress and completely kill off their influence. She and Ahab sought to control religious practices and beliefs as a means of securing power, maintaining social order, and political control. The prophets' messages condemned her actions and lifestyle, including her promotion of idol worship, manipulation of political power, and persecution of the followers of the God of Israel.

JEZEBEL STEALS INHERITANCE

We are all familiar with her disdain toward Elijah and her plot to destroy and kill him after his defeat of Baal and the prophets of Baal. In 1 Kings 21, we then learn of another deplorable act. Ahab desired to have Naboth's vineyard as his own.

> *Now Naboth the Jezreelite had a vineyard in Jezreel right by the palace of Ahab king of Samaria. And after this Ahab spoke to Naboth saying, "Give me your vineyard.... I will give you a better vineyard for it, or if you prefer, I will give you its worth in money"* (1 Kings 21:1-2 MEV).

Naboth refused to sell his birthright inheritance to the king. Ahab was upset and began to pout. Look at the depth of entitlement that is present when rulers aligned with demonic principalities are in power.

Jezebel his wife said to him, "Are you not the governor of the kingdom of Israel? Get up and eat bread, and let your heart be happy, for I will get the vineyard of Naboth the Jezreelite for you" (1 Kings 21:7 MEV).

It is important to state here that Ahab was weak. A Jezebel spirit and principality will look for someone weak to empower her agenda. We will discuss this below, but a Jezebel spirit can operate through a man or a woman.

JEZEBEL AND THE SONS OF BELIAL'S EVIL PLOT

Jezebel through her cruel abuse of power as queen set her depraved and evil plot to kill Naboth in motion to ensure that Ahab got what he wanted.

So she wrote letters in Ahab's name and sealed them with his seal and sent the letters to the elders and to the nobles that were in the city where Naboth lived. In the letters she wrote, "Proclaim a fast, and set Naboth on high among the people, and set two men, sons of Belial, before him, to bear witness against him, saying, 'You blasphemed God and the king.' And then carry him out and stone him, so that he will die" (1 Kings 21:8-10 MEV).

The sons of Belial are ones who are mentioned throughout the Old Testament. They were considered scoundrels and were ones who operated in deceit, accusation, and evil acts. *Belial* is defined as "wickedness, what does not conform to a right standard, of no worth, evil person, troublemaker, vile thing" (Strong's #H1100). Obviously, this spirit operating through these two evil and deceitful men partnered with Jezebel in her evil plot to kill Naboth. They carried it through without hesitation. Just to give two more examples, they also stood against David and his kingdom and stirred up strife and dissension between Israel and the tribe of Benjamin. This spirit is a destiny and inheritance robber and killer and will speak blatant lies and promote lawlessness through its demonic agenda.

JEZEBEL WANTS TO RULE OVER TIME

Let's delve deeper into the location of Naboth's vineyard. It is interesting that Jezreel means "God sows." Much occurred in the valley of Jezreel. The Israelites encamped here before battling the Philistines (1 Samuel 29). It was also one of the towns over which Ishbaal, son of Saul, briefly reigned (2 Samuel 2:9). As we have learned, Ahab and Jezebel had a royal residence here, and Naboth's vineyard was beside the palace. Jehu murdered Jezebel and the rest of the house of Ahab in the valley (2 Kings 9:30-37), putting an end to the Omride dynasty (2 Kings 10:1-11). It was also one of the inherited cities allotted to the tribe of Issachar, one of the twelve tribes of Israel, when the Israelites possessed the promised land.

The sons of Issachar also knew the timing of the Lord, *"Of the tribe of Issachar, men who understood the times, with knowledge of what Israel should do, two hundred chiefs; and all their relatives were at their command"* (1 Chronicles 12:32 AMP). They could accomplish with 200 what took other tribes very large numbers to achieve. They were men of great skill above any of their neighbors as they were men who had understanding of the times. The Hebrew word for *understanding* is *yada*. It means "to advise, answer, appoint, discern, perceive, know, comprehend, to have understanding, to be wise, have skill, and to be cunning" (Strong's #H3045). They exemplified ones who embodied keen discernment and prophetic insight in how to lead an entire nation and its divinely called leader into its new season and era of victory. Here are the ways the Lord gifted the sons of Issachar in this calling, which is in strong opposition to the Jezebel spirit.

Wisdom for the Harvest

They understood the natural times by discerning the face of the sky. They studied the movements of the stars and planets and understood chronological time. They were weather-wise, could advise in the proper times for plowing, sowing, and reaping. In other words, the processes to go through to reap a harvest!

Alignments to Assemble and Release Abundance

Through the aligning of the stars they knew the times to call the nation to assemble for the ceremonial times, the times appointed for the Jewish feasts. *"They will call the peoples to the mountain; there they will offer sacrifices of righteousness, for they will draw out the abundance of the seas and the treasures hid in the sand"* (Deuteronomy 33:19 MEV). This is a powerful example of bringing an entire nation together to worship in a sacred assembly as the Ekklesia in the appointed times and season. As a result, favor concerning provision and supply was realized.

Discernment in Advancing Peoples and Nations

The sons of Issachar excelled in knowledge and wisdom of the laws of God. As Israel moved through the wilderness, God chose the sons of Issachar as one of the three tribes to lead the way when the nation advanced. Judah, the ones of worship and war, went first. Then Issachar, the wise and discerning ones, would go second. Zebulun, the financiers and ones of supply, would go third. They had the ability to maneuver in discernment strategies to make a way for provision and supply.

Discernment to Support God's Appointed Leaders

They understood public affairs and political times, the disposition of the nation, and the tendencies of their unfolding events. In other words, the tribe had keen insight and made good use of it. They knew what Israel should do. From their wisdom and experience they learned both their own responsibilities and the duty and interest of others. In the critical time spoken of in 1 Chronicles, they knew Israel was to make David the King. In Judges 5:15, we read of "the princes of Issachar." As this part of their story testifies, they were with Deborah and Barak and went to battle under her leadership. Although at this time in history women did have some rights in Israel, it was still unusual for a woman to sit in authority over the nation. The sons of Issachar could discern the times and seasons and they knew God's hand was on her and it was her time to lead.

Anointed and Appointed to Lead

In Judges 10:1-2, we read of one of their own who rose to leadership as a judge, *"Tola, the son of Puah, the son of Dodo, a man of Issachar, arose to save Israel. …He judged Israel for twenty-three years"* (MEV). They knew when a leader was falling and a leader was rising. They could discern if they were to lead or who the next leader was to be and then lead by example in the following of him or her.

Jezreel is Kingdom of Heaven inherited land of the tribe of Issachar—the ones who played a significant role in leading the children of Israel. Ahab and Jezebel stole the rightful possession of this divinely allotted land. She wanted time in her hands and not the hands of the sons of Issachar. Interestingly enough, Issachar was actually conceived on the feast of harvest, which is the day we would know as Pentecost. Jezebel will stand in direct affront against a Pentecostal movement—a Holy Spirit baptism and fire encounter that awakens power and authority. She's a thief who robs inheritance. She is a manipulator keeping people out of God's timing by silencing the prophetic voice. She wants to kill assignments and strategies spoken and birthed by the Lord. She initiates schemes to kill and rob the fire and passion of the Lord.

THE LORD JUDGED AHAB AND JEZEBEL

Then the word of the Lord came to Elijah the Tishbite: "Go down to meet Ahab king of Israel…. He is now in Naboth's vineyard, where he has gone to take possession of it. Say to him, 'This is what the Lord says: Have you not murdered a man and seized his property?' Then say to him, 'This is what the Lord says: In the place where dogs licked up Naboth's blood, dogs will lick up your blood—yes, yours!'"

Ahab said to Elijah, "So you have found me, my enemy!"

"I have found you," he answered, "because you have sold yourself to do evil in the eyes of the Lord. He says, 'I am going to bring disaster on you. I will wipe out your descendants and cut off from Ahab every last male

in Israel—slave or free. …And also concerning Jezebel
the Lord says: 'Dogs will devour Jezebel by the wall of
Jezreel'" (1 Kings 21:17-21,23 NIV).

Whew! The Lord in His righteous anger meant business.
The story goes on to reveal that upon hearing these words,
Ahab tore his clothes, put on sackcloth, and humbled himself.
Therefore, the Lord relented and removed the disaster occurring
during Ahab's lifetime, but instead would occur in the time of his
sons. Jezebel did not relent or humble herself.

IT'S TIME FOR JEHU!

After Ahab's death and during the reign of his son Joram, Elisha
the spiritual son of Elijah sent a son of a prophet to anoint Jehu,
the commander of the king's army, as the new king of Israel. Jehu
then chased down and killed Joram, the son of Ahab and Jezebel.
Now it was time for Jehu to dethrone and conquer Jezebel. Jehu
rode into the valley of Jezreel to ensure the judgment of the Lord
was fulfilled as was prophesied through Elijah. Jezebel had stirred
up Ahab, and then her sons, to do wickedly. She was a cursed
woman. She was a curse to the country and her people. Her rule
had lasted through three reigns—that of her father, her husband,
and her son. But now her day to be dethroned had come.

In Chapter Two, the false prophet of Jezebel in the church
of Thyatira was discussed. It is the same portrayal that we
have learned about Jezebel and her reign as queen with King
Ahab—a seductress, seducing God's servants to idolatry. There
was an extended time for her to repent, yet no humility occurred.
Therefore, a dreadful end will be brought on the Jezebel of

Revelation (2:22-23), just as Jezebel, Queen of the Northern Kingdom of Israel. I believe the Lord acted in this manner so that it is clear that Jezebel's destruction may be looked upon as the divine consequence for idolaters and persecutors. Especially the great whore, the mother of harlots, that made herself *drunk with the blood of saints* and the nations *drunk with the wine of her fornications*. And God Himself shall put it into the heart of the kings of the earth to hate her and turn on her (Revelation 17:5-6,16).

As Jehu rode into Jezreel, Jezebel heard that Jehu had killed her son, Joram. His death was due to her evil, whoredom, witchcraft, idolatries, deceptions, and plotted killings and murders. Jehu had his dead body thrown into the land portion of Naboth that was stolen by her. I am sure she had the expectation that she would be next in line for Jehu's revenging sword.

Daring the impending judgment, she posted herself in a window at the entrance of the gate to affront Jehu. Instead of hiding, as one afraid of divine vengeance, she exposed herself to it, mocked at the fear of it. It is astonishing how evil hardens hearts to such a degree that even when the severe consequence of the sin is about to rendered, there is still the depraved mocking against our Heavenly Father. Instead of humbling herself and mourning for her son, she made herself beautiful so that she might appear as she always had—the seductive, powerful, great, and majestic queen.

There was no trembling before Jehu. Instead, she attempted to strike fear in him with her threatening question, "*Is everything all right, Zimri, murderer of his master*" (2 Kings 9:31 MEV). It really is not a new outcome for those who are doing the Lord's work to be looked upon as those who disrupt what has been called and disguised as peace. Active reformers, like Jehu, are oftentimes threatened by those who lead in the demonic swaying of cultures.

She quoted an instance from the past in asking, "*is everything all right, Zimri?*" This was a blatant insult and threat. Zimri was the shortest king to reign in the Northern Kingdom of Israel. He wickedly came to the throne by blood and treason and within seven days the capital city was assaulted by Omri, Ahab's father. Zimri and his troops surrendered quickly. He took his own life by burning the palace down around him, committing suicide by fire. Zimri acted merely on his own ambition and cruelty. Jehu was anointed by one of the sons of the prophets and was commissioned by order from the Lord. In discerning people and situations, it is necessary to carefully distinguish between the precious and vile to appropriately respond.

The attempt to deter Jehu did not succeed. He had been called and sent to do the Father's work in reforming the land and punishing those who had defiled it. He lifted up a standard and made a proclamation, "*Who is on my side?*" When reformation is called upon from the Lord, it is time to ask and know those who are on His side.

Her own attendants, eunuchs, delivered her to her death, immediately throwing her out of the window. If the Lord's command to Jehu was to secure Jezebel's dethroning and death, then they were also going to engage with this divine directive. It is not a far reach to believe that they probably had a secret dislike and hatred of Jezebel and her wicked treatment toward them, though they were forced to serve her. Whatever their motivation, Jezebel was dashed against the wall and the pavement, and then trampled by Jehu's horses. The dogs ate her flesh and all that remained was her skull, feet, and the palms of her hands.

To finish the work of cleansing the land of all defilement and evil, he secured the death of all of Ahab's sons, numbering 70, and all the prophets of Baal. *Jehu* means "Jehovah is he." He was a reformer, called to conquer the demonic rule of principalities over his people and the land. I believe as we have studied Jezebel, we can say we are witnessing this principality throughout our culture, nation, and the nations. We see distinct manifestations in the spheres of culture—education, business, government, media, arts and entertainment, the church. This is a now time for the Jehus to rise up! The called and chosen ones as an army of Jehus who are surrendered, abandoned, and bringing forth His Kingdom to see the Jezebel principality and spirit overthrown, defeated, and conquered!

REVISITING THE CHURCH OF THYATIRA

I know your deeds, and your love and faith and service and perseverance, and that your deeds of late are greater than at first. But I have this against you, that you tolerate the woman Jezebel, who calls herself a prophetess, and she teaches and leads My bond-servants astray so that they commit acts of immorality and eat things sacrificed to idols. I gave her time to repent, and she does not want to repent of her immorality (Revelation 2:19-21 NASB).

As stated in Chapter Two in our brief discussion about Jezebel, it is convicting to read that the Lord gave her time to repent. This leads to the reasoning that this admonition is not left only to dealing with a principality, but to individuals or leaders who choose to align with this principality, allowing its influence to work in and through them and who remain completely unrepentant. We as Christians and discerning believers have to walk in spiritual wisdom and understanding to determine the difference in effectiveness and operation of an individual demonized by a Jezebel spirit or a person operating under the influence of the principality of Jezebel. Therefore, it is imperative that we ensure nothing in our lives is tolerating and permitting Jezebel. Below is a brief list of symptoms if someone is individually under the influence of a Jezebel spirit. As a reminder, both men and women can be demonized by a Jezebel spirit.

1. Fear of rejection can be a root open door. Therefore, control and manipulation are exerted to protect from being hurt.

2. They target leaders and offer to serve while hiding their manipulative behavior from this leader, but not from others.

3. They make promises and commitments quickly.

4. They use the names of others with whom they have no relationship in order to impress.

5. They express themselves as super-spiritual to gain attention and acceptance.

6. They have their own agenda and are looking for disciples of their own.

7. They isolate and bring division between others to gain the upper hand.

8. They will lie, deceive, and accuse others.

9. They are seductive in nature.

10. They play the victim, will never admit wrong, and blame everyone else.

11. They play on others' compassion to sway discernment.

12. They feel and act entitled.

13. They function in false humility.

14. They shun true accountability and accuse others of having a Jezebel spirit.

15. They want to mentor hurt and wounded people.

16. They operate with a lot of insecurity.

17. They initiate witchcraft prayers to manipulate and curse others.

Personal Prayer

Father, thank You for Your truth that sets me free. Jesus, thank You that by Your blood and through Your Name, I'm forgiven, cleansed, and set free. Lord, I now confess and repent for myself and previous generations in my family bloodline concerning all involvement and engagement in or with the beliefs, submission to, worship, and practices of Jezebel.

I repent and ask that You forgive me for rejection and resulting manipulation in my life. I repent for deception and manipulation of leaders and those in close relationship and proximity to those leaders. I repent for all deception, lying, and accusation and the false using of names of prominent leaders in order to impress to gain unmerited favor. I repent for making false commitments. I repent for appearing super-spiritual to gain attention. I repent for all competition, jealousy, and selfish agendas of robbing of disciples and inheritance. I repent for all intentional division in churches, businesses, families. I repent for engaging in acts of seduction, playing the victim, and blaming others for the areas I struggle in instead of accepting personal responsibility. I repent for false humility and the belief of entitlement at the cost of others' reputation and kingdom inheritance. I repent for rejecting accountability and all false accusation of others having a Jezebel spirit. I repent for further wounding the wounded. I repent of insecurity and all witchcraft divination, word cursing of others, manipulation, and rebellion. Jesus, thank You that by Your blood and through Your name I am cleansed and forgiven.

I now renounce fear of rejection and the spirit of rejection. I renounce all trauma and resulting control and manipulation. I renounce actions of flattery, deception, and manipulation of leaders to impurely gain relationship. I renounce the deception of making commitments that will never be kept. I renounce the repeated pattern and actions of aggression, deception, and jealousy to control and intimidate others. I renounce the using of names in order to impress others to bring manipulated favor in my life.

I renounce the deception of being super-spiritual to gain attention and acceptance. I renounce having my own selfish agenda of recruiting disciples and preying on the wounded to bring further wounding. I renounce all isolation and the selfish and demonic attempt to divide others, churches, families, ministries, businesses, etc. I renounce all lies, deception, and accusation of others.

I renounce all seduction. I renounce the victim spirit and blaming of others. I renounce playing on others' compassion to sway discernment. I renounce all thoughts and actions of entitlement. I renounce false humility and the shunning of authority and accountability. I renounce all insecurity and witchcraft prayers to manipulate and curse others.

Now in the authority of Jesus, Jezebel spirit I renounce you and break your hold in my life. I command you to get out of my life! Your assignment is cancelled, null and void, and I am rendering you an eviction notice now!

Father, thank You for Your freedom. I rejoice that I am free indeed! Thank You, Lord, for purity, freedom, and victory in my life. Holy Spirit, every place where my house has been swept clean, fill me up to overflowing. I welcome and declare purity and holiness in my thoughts, mind, emotions, and desires. Lord, I declare that Your Word is alive in me. I ask for more of You in my life. Jesus, You are the Alpha, Omega, the Beginning and the End. You are the Magnificent One, the Holy One, the Redeemer of the World. You are Holy. All glory, power, and honor are due Your name! Amen.

Research Guidelines for Informed Intercession

It's time to engage in research to gain understanding and wisdom through the guided questions below. During this process, convening and holding corporate times of glory-anointed worship and intercession provides the atmosphere to subdue a Jezebel spirit in operation. In regions where the principality of Jezebel has been enthroned, convening unified assemblies and gatherings of churches and ministries is greatly effective. Intentional united times of worship, repentance, intercession, and prophetic declarations will begin to break through Jezebel's veil of darkness. In these gatherings, declared agreement with the prophetic words of destiny for spheres of influence and the region are powerful, victorious weapons of warfare.

1. Who were the foundational leaders of your region/ sphere of influence?

2. Were they believers?

3. If so, were they open to moves of the Holy Spirit?

4. Is the spirit of prophecy welcome and received?

5. Is there witchcraft manipulation in operation through prophetic voices in the region?

6. Is there a covenant-breaking spirit in operation? (A covenant-breaking spirit causes covenants between people groups to be broken and destroyed. It

will cause divorce, a lot of church splits, and disunity in churches in the region.)

7. Are there occult or witchcraft covens in your area who engage in worshipping an Asherah pole?

8. Did the original indigenous people in your region worship an Asherah pole?

9. Is there repeated sexual sin that is occurring within churches?

10. Is there repeated losing of finances, inherited blessings, or spiritual blessing?

11. Are there repeated patterns of a Jezebel spirit coming into churches to bring division?

12. Are there repeated patterns of strong, rebellious, and manipulative leaders in government?

13. Is it difficult to prophetically hear the voice of the Lord in your region?

14. What other forms of witchcraft and the occult are in operation?

15. Is there an occult movement of feminism, a strong representation of feminism that is aggressive and manipulative? If so, what spheres of society and culture has this movement impacted?

16. Have there been past moves of revival? If so, pray in agreement that those wells of revival will be awakened again.

17. How is the Lord moving now? Identify those areas and pray in agreement with the moves of His

Spirit. Intercede for more of His glorious presence, for revival and awakening.

18. Intercede for revival and awakening in the churches and spheres of culture and influence.

19. What are the prophetic and redemptive promises of the Lord?

20. What are His Kingdom strategies of stewardship of those words?

Chapter Eight

MAMI WATA

By Anthony Turner

Across Africa and the Caribbean, Mami Wata holds a central place in spiritual practices, rituals, and worship. She is venerated as a goddess of fertility, healing, and protection, invoked by fishermen seeking bountiful catches, women longing for children, and travelers embarking on perilous journeys. However, Mami Wata is also feared for her ability to lure mortals to their watery demise or to exact vengeance upon those who betray her trust.

In 2010, I was set free from a generational curse that I didn't even know was affecting my life. I was pastoring a thriving church in Colorado Springs that had an equally thriving missions ministry. We would take two to three short-term missions trips each year to various countries around the world to work with our full-time missionaries. We were blessed to have missionaries on five of the seven continents. I had the privilege of leading these teams. We as a church had a heart for the nations, so it was so wonderful to get to go to all of the places we went to bring the Kingdom. I'd never been to the continent of Africa even though we had several missionaries who work in various countries there. I, however, was not concerned by this because honestly I never had a desire to go. One of our long-term missionaries working there came home on furlough and in typical fashion we celebrated his time home by hosting a banquet. Our missionaries were honored at these banquets and also got the opportunity to share their experience with the church body.

On this occasion our missionary talked about his work in Benin. Benin is known as the birthplace of voodoo as well as one of Africa's slave ports. The missionary began to tell us of the day in the country that they set apart to take the visiting short-term teams on a field trip down the historical "slave road," where conquering tribes would sell the people of the defeated tribes to the slave traders for guns, flour, wine, and other items. Before boarding the ships, the conquering chief would perform a ritual around a tree known as the Tree of Forgetfulness in order to wipe the slaves' memories of their family, their tribe, and Africa. When the missionary shared this information with our church, I then realized why I never wanted to go to Africa; I was under a generational curse. When I uttered that out loud, the intercessors and ministry leaders of our church all came around me and broke the power of that bloodline curse off of my life. A few weeks later I was invited for the first time to come to Mali, Africa, to speak in a conference, which I accepted. It was one of the greatest experiences of my life. Little did I know at that time that this would be the beginning of a discovery nine years in the making.

I would share my testimony countless times over the years with many of my friends and colleagues. I would Google search the Tree of Forgetfulness, which would bring up pictures of where the tree once stood. There is a monument there now in Ouidah, Benin. I never gave much thought to it until I was sharing my testimony nine years later with another friend on the eve of a worship and prayer assignment I was asked to be a part of.

These on-site assignments were something that, for some reason, a couple of my friends and kingdom colleagues would invite me to join, to be a part of the team they were assembling. I never liked being invited on one of these land assignments. I knew it was necessary, but it was not my cup of tea; that's what my friend and author of this book, Becca Greenwood, was called to. So anytime I was asked, I would reluctantly say yes. The assignment I'm referring to above, where I had just shared my testimony, falls into the "You Can't Make This Stuff Up" category.

I'd been asked to be a part of a ten-day worship and prayer assignment that would go from the headwaters of the Mississippi River to the mouth. My friend called it Justice in the Waters. He was given the vision to do a worship and prayer strike along the Mississippi River to deal with water spirits—a subject of which I had no knowledge whatsoever. This validated my reluctancy to be a part of this assignment.

While at the hotel with my friend sharing my testimony, I Googled *Tree of Forgetfulness* once again as I'd done countless times before. Only this time I noticed that the monument that stands where the tree once stood was an image of some type of mermaid-like entity. I was speechless. After all of these times pulling that information up, I'd never noticed the image before. I immediately began researching the image to discover that it is the most venerated deity on the west coast and central Africa and also the African Diaspora. Her name is Mami Wata, and she is still worshipped across much of Africa today.

Nine years had passed from the time I got delivered from that African generational curse, and the next morning I was part of a team that was assigned with the task of dealing with water spirits in America. The ironic timing of the Lord was that this assignment was beginning June 19, 2019—a date that is celebrated by the black community in the United States as Juneteenth. This was the day that every slave in the U.S. was officially freed; 2019 was also the 400th anniversary of the first slave ship arriving in North America. Which means this was also the 400th anniversary of the arrival of Mami Wata to North America.

WHO IS MAMI WATA?

In the tapestry of African and Afro-Caribbean folklore, few figures loom as large as Mami Wata. She is a deity, a spirit, a force of nature, and a symbol of the complex interplay between tradition and modernity. Mami Wata's influence extends across continents and cultures, boundaries, and, through some recent incidents here in the US, is resurgent as the force that empowered the Black Lives Matter movement. Scholars trace her roots to ancient African water spirits. These spirits also are known as a syncretic figure, blending indigenous beliefs with elements of Christianity and other religions brought by colonial powers. Her depictions have been profoundly influenced by representations of ancient, indigenous African water spirits, European mermaids, Hindu gods and goddesses, and Christian and Muslim saints. She is not only sexy, jealous, and beguiling, but also exists in the plural as the mami watas and papi watas who comprise part of the vast and uncountable "school" of African water spirits.

Mami Wata traces back to the earliest of African societies as recorded by the griots and keepers of history. The Dogon's creation myth tells the stories of Mami Wata and traces records of its existence to more than 4,000 years ago. Mesopotamian myths also tell of the great water goddess in their story of creation, known as Mami Aruru, to be the creator of life.

The name is traced to the early languages of many modern African societies today. The first root of its name is considered to be from Ethiopian and Egyptian Coptic societies. In the Ethiopian Coptic language, the word *mama* was used as a description of truth and wisdom, and the term *uat-ur* meant ocean water. Another definition of the name traces to the early Sudanese society where the word *wata* referred to a woman. The name is often linked to a single entity but represents the strongest and most significant of all water spirits that exist.

Mami Wata, while predominantly known by this name, is known by many names, as she has been interwoven into the religions and the cultures of every people group where African slaves were sold. Some of the names she has taken on are indicative of the language and regions. Some of these alternative names and variations include:

- Mami Wata Nyama
- Maman de l'Eau

- Maman Dlo (in Haiti and the French Caribbean)
- Yemaya (associated with the Yoruba orisha in Afro-Cuban and Afro-Brazilian religions)
- La Sirene (in Haitian voodoo)
- La Balenn (in Haitian voodoo)
- Santa Marta la Dominadora (in syncretic traditions in Latin America)
- Yemanjá (in Brazilian Candomblé)
- Jengu (in Cameroonian traditions)
- Nana Buluku (in some West African traditions)
- Nana Densua (in Ghanaian Akan mythology)

In West Africa and some parts of Eastern Africa, the deity is called Mami Wata or Maame Wata. Modern African societies refer to her as Maame/Mami Wata. In some parts of Eastern Africa, among the Swahili speaking groups, she is called Mamba Munti.

These names and variations reflect the diverse cultural and regional interpretations of the water spirit, demonstrating her infiltration and significance across different spiritual practices and belief systems. In each one of these iterations of Mami Wata, she is known as the "Mother of All Water."

The people who inhabit the coastal region from Benin, Ghana, and Togo worship a vast pantheon of water deities, of which Mami Wata is most prominent. An entire hierarchy of the Mami Wata priesthood exists in this region to officiate ceremonies, maintain the shrines, conduct healing rituals, and initiate new priests and priestesses into the service of various Mami Wata deities.

On February, 15, 2020 at 9:00 AM in the city of Cotonou, Benin, a high priest of Vodou and Mami Wata named Hounnon Behumbeza was officially appointed the Supreme Chief of Mami Wata. As an indication of how revered Mami Wata is in the region, Hounnon Behumbeza's coronation as Supreme Chief of Mami Wata was broadcast live on various television news programs and featured in local newspapers. The coronation was attended by hundreds of priests from around the region and the highest dignitaries of Vodou and the Mami Wata tradition. Also in attendance were Benin Republic's minister of culture and several local government officials.

Mami Wata is the bigger goddess with smaller followers, some of which were also men and had the same appearance as their goddess. Stories are told of her followers coming to shore every now and then to deceive seamen and capture them to be taken in the water kingdom. The captives were a source of entertainment until they were offered as sacrifices to her.

WHAT ARE SOME CHARACTERISTICS OF MAMI WATA?

Mami Wata is depicted with a variety of characteristics across different cultural and regional interpretations. However, some common characteristics and attributes associated with Mami Wata include:

- Beauty: Mami Wata is often described as extraordinarily beautiful, with long flowing hair, captivating eyes, and an alluring presence that mesmerizes those who encounter her.

- Serpentine Features: In many depictions, Mami Wata exhibits serpentine characteristics, such as a serpent's tail, scales, or the ability to transform between human and serpentine forms. This association with serpents symbolizes her connection to water, fertility, and the mysteries of the deep. In art and pictures she is often seen with two pythons—one wrapped around her waist with its head between her breasts and one she holds over her head.

- Association with Water: Mami Wata's primary domain is water, including rivers, lakes, and oceans. She is often depicted emerging from or residing within bodies of water, symbolizing her control over its currents and inhabitants.

- Fertility and Prosperity: Mami Wata is frequently associated with fertility, abundance, and prosperity. She is believed to bestow blessings upon her devotees, granting them wealth, success, and good fortune in various aspects of life.

- Healing Powers: Mami Wata is also revered for her healing abilities. Followers may invoke her for assistance in curing illnesses, easing childbirth, or providing protection from harm.

- Dual Nature: Mami Wata embodies both benevolent and capricious qualities, reflecting the dualities of life and nature. While she can be generous and nurturing toward her devotees, she is also capable of exacting punishment or causing misfortune to those who disrespect her or violate her taboos.

- Association with Luxury and Material Wealth: Mami Wata is often depicted adorned with jewelry, pearls, and other symbols of luxury and material wealth. This association underscores her role as a patron of prosperity and abundance.
- Cross-Cultural Appeal: Mami Wata's worship and influence extend beyond specific ethnic or cultural boundaries even in modern-day culture. She is worshipped by diverse communities across Africa and the African diaspora, as well as in syncretic religious practices that blend indigenous beliefs with elements of Christianity and other traditions.

As stated in the last characteristic, Mami Wata has been woven into every aspect of culture and there has been a resurgence of the worship of Mami Wata even in the US. In 2020, when many of our cities were being destroyed and statues were being torn down, much of this was being incited by groups such as Occupy, Antifa, and BLM. Black Lives Matter was founded by three women from the LGBTQ community who also stated that they are trained Marxists. They organized chapters in 16 major cities of the US and started protests in many cities under the guise of social justice. They were backed by politicians, the media, the entertainment community, and many professional athletes. They would especially rally protesters after a police shooting. The protesters would arrive at the site where blood was shed. The BLM organizers would then build a memorial (which was an altar), pour out libations on behalf of the person whose blood was shed, and the protesters would be instructed to "Say his name" or "Say her name." The crowd would begin chanting the name of the person who was killed.

Many people ignorantly thought that this was simply to honor the person killed, but in fact the three co-founders of BLM were not only Marxist, but priestesses of the African religion Odu Ifa, which believes in ancestral worship and conjuring the spirits of the dead. This is the exact ritual in which the ancestors, also known as the Igu, were conjured. One of the main deities worshipped in this religion is Mami Wata. This is the same deity that Haiti credits for allowing them to gain their independence. They claimed that they would summon Mami Wata so they could be filled with her rage. I believe this spirit of rage was released over our nation in 2020 as thousands of people chanted at altars erected at sites where blood was shed in order to conjure spirits to establish rage and chaos in this nation. In several places in our nation, Mami Wata statues have been built. For example, in New Orleans a statue of Robert E. Lee was taken down and in its place a statue of Mami Wata was erected.

I have discovered that so many people of African descent in this nation are still operating in the worship of this water spirit without being aware. There are so many things we have woven into our culture that we've seen as benign and harmless but continue to open doors to be imprisoned by a generational curse. I've begun personally asking the Lord to reveal things that I've integrated into my life that have their origin in the worship of other gods.

This is now the time to close *all* doors that give the enemy access to our destiny. I believe the overt reemergence of Mami Wata is actually the grace and love of the Father letting us know the things that have been hiding and lurking in our bloodline and keeping us from our Kingdom destiny. The erecting of these altars is intended to call out to those latent generational sins to pull us back into the things the blood of Jesus was shed to deliver us from.

One of the prophetesses of Mami Wata worship, known as Mama Zogbé, who lives here in the United States, shows how Mami Wata has infiltrated other religions. She has written several books on this entity and has campaigned the black community to return to their ancestral roots and go back to the worship of Mami Wata.

In her book entitled *The Sibyls: the First Prophetess' of Mami (Wata): The Theft of African Prophecy by the Catholic Church*, Mama Zogbe states:

> For 6,000 years, Africa was ruled by a powerful order of Sibyl matriarchs. They produced the world's first oracles, prophetess and prophets. known as "Pythoness," they worked the oracles in the Black Egyptian colonies in ancient Greece, Rome, Turkey, Israel, Syria and Babylon. Their holy temples were more numerous than the churches of today. In ancient Rome, they first established the "holy seat" of the Vatican advising the world's

heads of state. Centuries before Christ, they cured epileptics, the blind, lepers and "casted out demons." It was a Sibyl who called-up the spirit of "Apostle" Samuel. Their "pagan" prophecies were used by the emerging Roman papals to create a "western theological" foundation and became the undisputed precursor for their Christian Bible. African women's religious history is finally being unearthed, exposing shocking revelations buried for more than 2000 years."[1]

If while reading this chapter you were convicted by the Holy Spirit and you want to renounce this from your bloodline, I have included a renunciation prayer for you to pray.

Personal Prayer

> Dear Heavenly Father, I repent on behalf of myself and my ancestors for turning to false gods, idols, cults, and all forms of idolatry. I repent for rebellion to You, and I turn away from all worship and false religious practices. Therefore:
>
> I renounce Mami Wata, who calls herself the Mother of All Waters; who sets herself as a usurper over the waters and commits fornication with the kings of this world; and whose wine of fornication I was made drunk with. I come out from you and your intoxicating lure.
>
> I renounce Oshun, the love goddess who rules sexuality and pleasure, also money matters, also known as Our

Lady of la Caridad del Cobre, patroness of Cuba, Our Lady of Charity, and the Virgin Mary.

I renounce Ymoja, the river goddess that rules over women and children, also known as Ymanja, Yemaya, Star of the Sea, the Virgin Mary, Our Lady of Regla, and other names associated with Mary and the African Mother goddess.

I renounce all covenants, rituals, and sacrifices made to spirits of darkness.

I renounce all enforcer spirits and command them to leave me in Jesus' name.

I renounce all soul ties to former lovers, shamans, witch doctors, sorcerers, and those they have worked through. Let all fragmented parts of my soul return to me, and any part of other people's souls return to them.

I apply the blood of Jesus Christ to every sin that has been committed by me and my ancestors, closing the door to these spirits and the assignments that they have had against me. I renounce all lying spirits, all trickery, manipulation, fraudulent practices intended to deceive and rob others. Please forgive me, Father, for all the things I have done that brought evil, pain, and suffering into the lives of others. Let the blood of Jesus cleanse me from all unrighteousness.

I repent for the sins of shedding blood, human and animal sacrifice, selfishness, rebellion, jealousy, contention, evil speaking, pride, and every sin that was caused by disobedience and rejecting the Lordship of Christ. Let the blood of Jesus cover these sins in Jesus' name.

I renounce all evil inheritances, both in the natural and the spiritual realm.

Let my name now be removed from every ungodly altar and the evil altar destroyed in Jesus' name.

Let every demon that has been assigned to carry out a curse be cut off and sent back to the abyss created for them in Jesus' name.

Let the fire of God burn up every evil work in my life. Let the conviction of God's Holy Spirit keep me from reopening an old door that has now been closed in Jesus' name.

Let the angelic hosts of heaven be assigned to fight on my behalf and release my restoration, in Jesus' name.

I forgive all those who have been an instrument in satan's service to cause pain, hardship, or ruin to me and my family. I also forgive myself for anything I have done that has brought guilt, shame, or condemnation upon myself.

I ask You, Father, to bless those who have cursed me or treated me wrong. I cancel their debt and forgive their sin in Jesus' name.

Father, I stand upon the principle of James 4:6-7. Now that I am submitted to Your authority, I command the enemy to take everything he has done to perpetuate a curse and leave me now in Jesus' name. I command every evil spirit that has been attached to my life to go back to the abyss in Jesus' name.

I also command the thief to repay the losses of previous years with no less than a sevenfold return according to Proverbs 6:31. I thank You for restoration, healing, and revival to my heart and life, Lord, in Jesus' name, amen.

Research Guidelines for Informed Intercession

Now that we have welcomed the delivering work of the Lord in our lives, let's apply what we have learned and investigate and discover the ways Mami Wata has impacted the regions and spheres of influence the Lord is highlighting for strategic assignments. As this process for victorious breakthrough begins, seek His guidance on convening corporate gatherings of worship, intercession, and reconciliation. Prayer-walk the area where there have been murders and death on which libations and incantations have occurred. Break the power of death and speak and proclaim healing and life into the land. Seek Holy Spirit concerning the prophetic acts to be done on the land to break the enemy's grip and to release healing, blessing, peace, and life. Pray for revival, awakening, and transformation to sweep through the people, land, and region.

1. Are there active chapters of Black Lives Matter, Antifa, or Occupy in the region?

2. Are these organizations impacting the spheres of influence in the region?

3. Was slavery prevalent in the region? If so, now that there is understanding about Mami Wata, was her worship perpetuated during that time?

4. Are there forms of witchcraft and the occult that revere and worship Mami Wata?

5. Have there been ceremonies from Black Lives Matter, Antifa, or Occupy on murder sites in the region?

6. Has the ritual of pouring out libations and saying his/her name been performed?

7. Are there any Mami Wata statues in the region?

8. In the history of the region, is there occult activity or conjuring of water spirits?

9. Are there active Odu Ifa worship meetings or gatherings?

10. Have local governmental leaders celebrated or empowered Mami Wata?

11. Have there been past moves of revival? If so, pray in agreement that those wells of revival will be awakened again.

12. How is the Lord moving now? Identify those areas and pray in agreement with the moves of His Spirit. Intercede for more of His glorious presence, for revival and awakening.

13. Intercede for revival and awakening in the churches and spheres of culture and influence.

14. What are the prophetic and redemptive promises of the Lord?

15. What are His Kingdom strategies of stewardship of those words?

Chapter Nine

THE KNIGHTS TEMPLAR

Brandon Larson

For many, just the sound of the name, Knights Templar, elicits all sorts of thoughts and imagery of mounted medieval warriors with red Jerusalem crosses emblazoned on their clean white tunics charging into battle. But who were these "warrior monks" as they were called, and how does their legacy impact us even to this day? And how do the Knights Templar relate to the Queen of Heaven? Let's take a brief look into this legendary group and examine these questions together.

CHIVALRIC MILITARY ORDER

The Knights Templar were a Catholic chivalric military order tasked with defending the Christian pilgrims traveling through-out medieval Europe on their way to the Holy Land and grew to become one of the largest and wealthiest organizations of its time. At the height of their power, they were the largest non-nation landowner in Europe and had castles and fortresses from Ireland to Scandinavia, Russia to Spain, Italy to Jerusalem. The extent of their wealth reached far beyond territorial holdings. However, their many castles held vast amounts of monetary wealth that surpassed any nation-state in Europe, and all of their vast holdings were defended by their well-trained professional knights revered as the finest soldiers of their day.

With the fall of Jerusalem to the Crusader armies in 1099, European Christians of all social levels could make a pilgrimage to the Holy Land and receive all manner of spiritual rewards, the least of which was the forgiveness of their sins. This led to a massive flow of pilgrims making the long journey from Europe to the Crusader States in the Holy Land.

Of course, travel was not an easy thing during this period. It was long, arduous, and very dangerous. There wasn't a Holiday Inn Express in every town, no gas stations, and often only the remnants of the old Roman roads remained connecting the many towns and villages. This led to a real problem for the many pilgrims on their journeys, with highway robbery and outright murder being commonplace.

Thus, the creation of the Knights Templar was founded in 1119 by a group of French nobles from the Champagne region, led by Hugh de Payns in response to the dire need for a system of protection for those making a pilgrimage to the Holy Land. Hugh recruited many Knights to his cause to create a brotherhood sworn as their holy duty before God to defend the pilgrims. Naturally, this was met with great enthusiasm and the Knights began to grow and were given many estates and castles to assist in their mission to defend the pilgrims. This growing support led to King Baldwin II of Jerusalem granting to the Templars a valuable section on the Temple Mount to use as their headquarters, securing their standing as one of the most prominent organizations in all of Christendom, and positioning them for their future growth. And so, the Knights Templar, or *Poor Fellow-Soldiers of Christ and of the Temple of Solomon*, as they were called at the time, were born.

The fact that the Knights had a home on the Temple Mount has led to one of the more intriguing stories of the Templars. As the story goes, while digging under their headquarters on the Temple Mount, the Templars allegedly found some secret knowledge or secret relics buried under their new home. Everything from the Holy Grail to the Ark of the Covenant, or even a trove of ancient scrolls with hidden mysteries, has been listed throughout the years as the secret found by the Templars and has given way to many conspiracy theories and outlandish stories about the Templars. The historical accuracy of any discovery is of course lost to history and dubious at best. What is likely true is that from their home on the Temple Mount, the Templars had influence and, with it, access to the different cultures and peoples of their day.

From its inception, the Knight Templars fashioned themselves as both warriors and pious monks or priests. It was this dual role and dual identity that was at the core of their order and at the core of their belief systems. The Knights Templar were priests, or monks, dedicated to strict daily religious practices first and foremost before they were warrior knights.

From their earliest days as a Catholic military order, they found a great champion in Bernard of Clairvaux, the founder of the Cistercian monastic order and one of, if not the most powerful man within the Catholic Church at this time. Bernard was the nephew of one of the founding members of the Templars, and was all too willing to throw his support behind the order, going as far as to even co-author their founding principles now known as the "Latin Rule."

Bernard lent his full support to the Templars and was their biggest advocate throughout his life, molding and shaping the order, both religiously and politically, through his influence upon the pope and thus the rest of Europe. This culminated in 1139 when Bernard successfully secured a papal bull (official decree of the pope) called *Omne Datum Optimum,* which established the Knight Templars as an autonomous organization answerable only to the pope himself and exempt from all other political or religious authority across all Christendom. Now the Templars could grow unimpeded by any other authority in the land. And grow they did, amassing wealth, castles, lands, fleets, and adding to their number all over the western world.

Over the next 200 years or so, the Templar Order became a dominant player in the socio-political and economic world. As their power grew and their ranks swelled with young men from the aristocratic families of Europe, the Templars' religious beliefs began to change and to take on a very distinct set of doctrines separate from those more commonly taught in the wider Catholic Church. Remember, the Templars were at their core both warriors and priests/monks. They fully embraced this dual identity and devoted most of their daily life to monostatic traditions established by Bernard of Clairvaux.

However, we can see in their teaching and their history a willingness to extend their beliefs beyond the traditional orthodox beliefs of the Catholic Church. They had an extreme reverence for the Virgin Mary, something they learned from Bernard, who himself was an ardent and some say radical worshipper of the Virgin Mary. We can see that Mary worship was ingrained in their order from its earliest day, thanks to Bernard, and was a foundational belief of the Templars.

Bernard's devotion and worship of Mary is well documented. He once said, we "cannot admire her enough."[1] This is the origin of the saying *"De Maria numquam satis,"* meaning "Of Mary there is never enough," which is attributed to Bernard by many, including Pope Pius XII.[2] Bernard's exaltation of the Virgin Mary was so well-known that Dante chose Bernard to sing the heavenly praises of Mary in *Canto 33* of his *Paradiso*, speaking of her as "humble and more exalted than any creature." It is safe to say that Bernard's personal devotion and love for the Virgin Mary were central to his life and to his teachings, which formed the core religious beliefs of the Knights Templar Order at its inception. So much so, that the Templars were instructed that new members should make their vows to "God and Our Lady," meaning the Virgin Mary.

OCCULT AND MYSTICAL SPIRITUAL INFLUENCES

Because of their deep roots in the Holy Land and regular interaction with Muslim inhabitants of the Crusader States, the Templars were heavily influenced by the belief system of Islam, particularly

Sufi Islam. Sufism is a sect of Islam and teaches a more mystical form of Islam, along with gnostic beliefs that were popular at the time in North Africa. One of the accusations against the Templars was that they were Muslim sympathizers, or that they had given in to Muslim beliefs. Contemporary writings about the Templars do show that at the time, the Templars did have good relations with some Muslims and were respectful of their beliefs. There are even instances in the Spanish peninsula where the Templars fought alongside the Muslims against fellow Christians when it suited their own goals. This is not to say that the Templars were Muslims or embraced Islam; rather, they were heavily influenced by Islam, especially the more gnostic Sufi Islam.

Likewise, there was close and regular interaction with the Jewish populations in the Holy Land, which led to an introduction to the Kabbalistic beliefs of Judaism finding its way into Templar belief systems. We can see this in the mixing of imagery and iconography used by the Templars in the many churches they built all over Europe. Rosslyn Chapel in Scotland, for example, though not built by the Templars but likely built by some of their descendants, is filled with a mix of imagery of both Christianity and Judaism.

Interestingly, there is a manuscript of the Templars Code (Latin Rule) at the National Library in Paris once owned by Godfrey of Saint-Victor (1125–c.1190), which is bound together with other manuscripts that include Jewish concepts, particularly the Tetragrammaton—the secret, unpronounceable four-letter name of God: YHWH. This was something not being used in Catholic teachings of the time. Godfrey of Saint-Victor himself was branded a heretic and forced out of his abbey before seeking refuge with the Templars.

These mystical spiritual beliefs of Kabbalah and Sufism were blended into the monastic system of the Templars and blended with the Cistercian teachings and Mary worship to create a unique blend of Catholicism within the Templar Order.

One of the earmarks of monastic orders during this time was secrecy, and much of what the Templars did was done behind the closed doors of their many castles and fortresses. This hidden life of the Templars created a prime breeding ground for occult and mystic practices and beliefs to flourish. More than that, it certainly fed the imagination of non-Templars at the time, even to this day. Just what were these pious, Christ-loving warrior monks doing in secret behind the doors of their many castles?

The Templars were master builders and built many churches and cathedrals all over Europe. They had carefully crafted expertise in the construction of these magnificent structures, which remain to this day as a testament to their skills. Their understanding of architecture and especially acoustics was spectacular.

This was one of the hallmarks of the Templar church—the ability to achieve specific and deliberately crafted acoustics that would allow for someone to position themselves at one singular spot and be able to speak, allowing the natural acoustics of the architecture to amplify their voice as if broadcast over a modern PA system. Stepping even a few inches in one direction or another, the amplification would stop, like magic if you will.

I have personally experienced this effect at numerous Templar churches, something that I have also experienced in ancient Egyptian temples, built thousands of years before the Templars. Perhaps they did find some ancient knowledge on the Temple Mount. I can't say, but one thing is clear, their understanding of acoustics and architecture was immense. How they utilized this knowledge and skill was concerning.

The amplification effect was not just in volume but also in frequency. By creating precise frequencies audibly through chanting and vocalization the sound would be "felt" as much as it was "heard."

During a time when all manner of unexplained things were considered "magical," imagine how much influence the Templars could have on the masses and the Masses when they employed their advanced knowledge of acoustics. It was like a false Holy Spirit, or a false anointing, to be able to speak or chant and have the congregation be impacted by the sounds physically as much as audibly.

TIME STANDS STILL

During one of our prayer journeys with Becca, we had an encounter with a practitioner of esoteric beliefs, which he believed were passed down from the Templars and those "in the know" as he put it. Inside a Templar church, below the remains of a Templar castle, around the last remaining original Templar altar in Spain, this individual shared much of those beliefs with us. Much of what he shared aligned with our research of the Templars' practices. Below is Becca's written report of the supernatural moment in time.

The year was 2013. I was leading a team of eight awesome prayer warriors to the nation of Spain. Over the past 20 years we have driven thousands of miles across the peninsula praying for revival, breakthrough, and transformation. The focus of this assignment was to pray from France, across Spain, into Portugal along the path of empowerment established by the Knights Templar. The purpose was to engage at key strategic locations where they practiced occult forms of worship and caused immense bloodshed through warfare to empower the idolatrous structures they revered. How did we know this was our assignment? The Lord specifically spoke to us that 2014 was the time to address the foundation of the banking system that was and still is influencing financial institutions in the world.

One key location we were to visit was the ancient castle in the beautiful, historic, sleepy town of Miravet. As is normal, all the castles were built on high places. After praying, we looked over the city from that high place and prophesied, calling in a harvest of souls as there are no Christian churches in this town. We also called for the release of hidden wealth. The Lord highlighted the steeple of an old cathedral and we knew we were to pray there. Some walked down the steep trail to the center of town while I along with Brandon and Kate Larson drove the van.

Arriving at the parking lot, we exited the van to proceed to the cathedral. However, I saw an advertisement that pictured Magnum ice cream bars. For me this has proven to be a great temptation. No discussion needed! Instead of walking uphill to the cathedral, I instantly made my way into the store to make my purchase. The gentleman behind the counter, Aurelio, welcomed us with a warm smile and began communicating in Spanish. I am able to speak a few words in Spanish, but I am not fluent. Yet when he spoke, I was supernaturally able to respond almost fluently. Soon, it was evident that this was paving the way for a friendly conversation to ensue. After a few minutes of "Spanglish," the rest of the team made their way into the entrance of the store, explaining that the cathedral doors were locked.

The owner of the store inquired, "Are you wanting to visit the new or the old cathedral?"

In unison we responded, "The old cathedral." He explained it was not open for tours. Taking the opportunity of my newfound friendship, I shared we were only visiting Miravet that day and were highly interested in visiting this ancient site. "Is there someone you know who could help us gain access?"

He responded, "You must know the keeper of the keys."

This quickly caused our prophetic ears to come to attention. Feeling the leading of the Holy Spirit, I asked, "Do you know the keeper of the keys?"

Smiling, he replied, "Yes. I am the keeper of the keys."

Excitement and laughter began to break out among the team as I took the opportunity to step further into our newfound favor, "Will you take us to the cathedral?" He gladly agreed, but we would have to wait thirty minutes allowing him time to close the store for siesta. Aurelio learned we had not eaten lunch and made a reservation with a restaurant in town for 3:15 p.m. to follow the tour. As we began the journey on the uphill road leading to the cathedral, the time was 2:20 p.m.

It was quickly evident that he was not only a store owner and the keeper of the keys, but also a top-notch historian. I must state that when you are obedient and step out in faith, our Father will ensure you relate to the right person, at the right place, at the right time. However, what should have been a ten-minute walk turned into thirty minutes as he shared the history of every block and building. When we arrived at the cathedral and made our way through the now unlocked and opened door. Brandom and I glanced at our watches. It was 2:55 p.m. I thought all plans for our lunch appointment would be foiled. We exchanged glances acknowledging the situation. However, both of us having been in supernatural experiences knew this was a divine setup. Therefore, we did not voice our concern; we allowed what we sensed was a supernatural divine encounter to unfold.

The inside of the cathedral was dusty, old, dilapidated. It had been through many battles without repair. Aurelio soon directed his conversation and attention to the front of the room. In the center of the altar was an old stone table. He invited all eight of us to gather around. He shared, "I feel I need to tell you things I do not normally share. You look as if you are people in the know, so I will tell you what I know." Expectantly we all leaned over the stone altar, pressing closer to listen. He proceeded to share the history of the Knights Templar in the region, information about their occult practices, and their involvement in sacred geometry. The altar we were circling was the only remaining occult altar of the eight Knights Templar altars used in the ancient Iberian Peninsula before they were disbanded by the King of France in 1312. Many of the Templars were welcomed into London and fled to that city. In time, several returned to collect all eight altars. They were able to locate seven but were unable to find the one housed in Miravet. The townspeople did not want to give up this sacred relic and retrieved it from the castle. They moved it into the cathedral, and it has been hidden since that time.

In recent history, the Templars had learned of the altar's location. Instead of moving it to the museum in London where the other seven altars are displayed, the decision was made to leave it in Miravet, its town of origin. However, in February of 2014, a group of high-ranking Knights Templar, those who are "in the know," had returned to reactivate the power of the altar. Due to his trusted position as keeper of the keys, our friend, Aurelio, was invited to witness the occult ritual. He explained what occurred at midnight on that night. The occult ceremony included chanting in a demonic sound to reactivate the witchcraft empowerment of the altar to influence Miravet, the nation of Spain, and the nations of the world. This occult brotherhood believes that in their occult magic powers they can produce wealth and metals in the atmosphere through the sound of their chanting. This is known as alchemy and is a practice in which the ancient principality of Hermes is invoked. It is also their intent to manipulate time, causing it to stand still to accomplish victory in battles and fulfill all the tasks necessary to control wealth. Friends, these practices are evil and demonic. I know this sounds a little "out there," but all these revelations I am sharing with you are historically and factually accurate. Jareb, a team member, planned for several of us to speak with the highest-ranking active Knights Templar who is also a highly respected historian. He travels and speaks about the history and practices of this organization. All of what I am sharing in this testimony he openly shared with us to be true.

The team was now beyond excited. We had been sent on assignment to another nation to pray and contend against the power of this system influencing the wealth in the world. The Lord so orchestrated our steps that we were now standing around the only ancient active altar of this occult group. To make a long story shorter, several of our team members were able to pray around that altar while several of us continued to speak to Aurelio in another room. Before leaving the cathedral, Aurelio expressed his desire to give us a gift. He positioned himself in front of that occult altar and began to beautifully sing an ancient Latin chorus, glorifying the magnificence and holiness of God. This moment was a divine setup which paved the way for me to offer Aurelio a gift. I too positioned myself in front of the demonic altar. As a worship warfare act to break the power of the demonic sound that had been released from that altar, I sang "Amazing Grace." The tangible glory of God fell in that temple and the darkness of that ancient stronghold was broken. Aurelio along with each of the team members and I wept tears in His glorious presence.

After our lengthy time in the cathedral, it was time for him to return to the store. As we departed, I glanced at my watch, feeling confident that we had missed our lunch appointment. To my utter surprise the time was 3:00 p.m. Could it really be possible that only five minutes had passed? Surely this wasn't right. Brandon was also in the same evaluating process. Without speaking a word, we both knew what had just occurred. We arrived at the restaurant exactly on time at 3:15 p.m. I waited until the team was seated at the table. There was much excitement concerning the miracle of the Lord making a way for us to pray at an altar when two hours before we had no knowledge of its existence. I asked the team members to look at their watches and share the time. They gladly obliged. I then explained, "When we walked into that cathedral it was 2:55 p.m. When we walked out it was 3:00 p.m. Time just stood still for us." Jareb then replied, "Becca, when I realized the full history lesson we were receiving from Aurelio I decided to record him. The time of the recording on my tablet is 45 minutes." Weeping broke out across that table. When you are anointed for an assignment in the glory realm and you receive His strategies, He will be with you in every step from the beginning to the end. Trust me, He will get you to the right place at the right time to ensure the assignment is completed through to victory.[3]

This ended up being one of the most remarkable experiences I have ever had. Time had literally and verifiably stood still for us. We entered a place of timelessness.

I believe the Lord orchestrated our time with this individual to give us key insight both into the Templars and into the fact that there are still those who believe and are actively seeking to use and tap into the Templars' demonic, occult beliefs.

BANKING

During the mission of the Templars to protect the pilgrims on their way to the Holy Land, the Templars found another way to assist the pilgrims, which would prove to be very profitable for them. To make the long journey you needed to have money to spend along the way. Typically, this meant carrying all the gold and silver you would need with you, but that would make you a prime target for highway robbery.

The Templars had a solution—bring your gold and silver to us and "deposit" it with us, and in return, we will give you a letter acknowledging your deposit. Then you can bring your letter to the next Templar castle along your journey, and we will let you "withdraw" a portion of your money that you deposited previously as evidenced by the letter you carried. Yes, the Templars created the modern banking system we all know and use to this day. The Templar castles and fortresses served as primitive "banks" for the many pilgrims, rich and poor, to safeguard their money and limit their vulnerability to robbery as they traveled. Of course, this valuable service came at a cost, which allowed the Templars to increase their wealth exponentially. Plus, now that they had so much wealth in their possession, they were able to also offer loans to the aristocracy of Europe, backed by the vast amounts of wealth they had stored in their castles.

The Templar banking system was the first of its kind and directly led to the modern concepts of deposits, cash withdrawals, bank loans, and even checks. If you needed to pay for an item but didn't have the money with you on hand, you could write a letter authorizing the Templars to give to the recipient the cash you had on deposit with them. In essence, you could write them a "check." Again, all done for a nominal fee of course.

Naturally, this was a very profitable service and led to the vast amounts of wealth the Templars amassed between their founding in 1119 and their official end in 1309. It likely is what led to their eventual demise. Eventually, the Templars were the wealthiest and largest player in Europe, and they had a lot of influence and control over the other nations of that time.

But even for the Templars, all good things must come to an end. By the beginning of the 14th century, much of Europe was dependent on and in debt to the Templars. Even the pope was beginning to get concerned about their power and influence. Something had to change. King Philip II of France, himself heavily indebted to the Templars to fund his country, decided he would be the one to bring about that change. He conspired with the pope and most of the other rulers of Europe at the time, and on Friday the 13th of October, 1307, throughout most of Europe there was a mass arrest of the Templars. They besieged their many castles and arrested as many Templars as they could find.

The official basis for this attack on the Templars was an accusation of all manner of heresy and unrighteous and unholy acts allegedly perpetrated by the Templars. King Philip and his supporters accused the Templars of everything from sorcery to homosexuality and were able to get the pope to officially renounce the order. Over the next few years, the few Templars who were arrested were subject to all the evils of their day as they were brought under the inquisition and tortured until they confessed to all the charges, whether they were true or not. This led to the official end of the order in 1314 when the pope dissolved them by papal bull called the *Vox in excelso* at the Council of Vienne.

Interestingly, not every European power supported the mass arrest. Portugal, for example, welcomed the Templars and simply had them change their name to the Order of Christ, which continued to flourish for years to come in Portugal. The Scottish nobility likewise welcomed the Templars and many immigrated to Scotland to find refuge there. Perhaps the largest contingent of displaced Templars, countless thousands fled to the Swiss Alps and settled into the many independent city-states that made up what would become modern-day Switzerland. Interestingly, Switzerland to this day is renowned for its banking tradition and global influence, a heritage stemming from their Templar roots.

Now, in all likelihood, King Philip expected that with the mass arrests and capture of the Templars' castles, he would gain huge amounts of wealth and seize all the gold and silver the Templars were storing inside. However, upon capturing their castles, he found relatively little wealth inside, nothing like what he expected. This has fueled countless legends and stories of the lost Templar treasure. Where did it go? Furthermore, despite their efforts to arrest all the Templars, only about 10 to 20 percent of the known Templars were likely arrested. The vast majority escaped, and with them the majority of the Templar wealth along with all of the spiritual practices.

WHAT DOES IT ALL MEAN?

So let's recap a little. The Knights Templar grew into a powerful and wealthy order of warrior priests who blended mystical religious beliefs into a new, distinct religion practiced in secret in their many castles. They invented the first banking system and used that to grow their wealth and exert influence and control over medieval Europe, which eventually led to their downfall.

First and foremost, the Knights Templar venerated the Virgin Mary at least as equal to Christ and spread that devotion throughout their domains. They learned this first from Bernard of Clairvaux and built it into their guiding rules and beliefs.

One of the other accusations at their trial, likely based on some degree of fact, was that the Templars worshipped Baphomet, the half-human, half-goat demonic entity. We know the word *Baphomet* was used by the Templars, but we have little evidence of what exactly was meant by the word. Keep in mind the image of Baphomet as the goat-headed demon wasn't created until 1865 when the "Sabbatic Goat" image was first drawn by Éliphas Lévi, a French occultist. Before this, there wasn't a context for Baphomet as a goat-headed demon.

Recently, a new theory has been presented by Dr. Hugh Schonfield, one of the original researchers working on the Dead Sea Scrolls. Schonfield decided to apply the Atbash cipher, which assisted with translating the Dead Sea Scrolls, to the Templars' sources with the word *Baphomet*. When he did, the word was translated as "Sophia" in Greek, which would translate into "Wisdom" in English. According to this theory, it could be argued that the Templars were worshipping Sophia, the goddess of wisdom who has been described as the bride of God. Given their strong veneration for the Queen of Heaven, it stands to reason they would have been open to venerating another form of the Queen of Heaven as Sophia.

One of the most interesting legacies of the Knights Templar can be found in another equally controversial group, the Freemasons. Much of the lore and created history that makes up Freemasonry is rooted in the Knights Templar. Freemasonry embodies many of the same ideals and even purports to carry on the Templar traditions and beliefs. There is an entire branch of Freemasonry and a corresponding Degree of Freemasonry called the Knights Templar (Freemasonry). The top Templar historian, whom Becca and Jareb spoke with before our 2013 Spain assignment, explained that true Knights Templar come into Freemasonry and ascend through the degrees of initiation for the sole purpose of induction into the Templar degree. Today, one can barely do a Google search or try and do any research on one without getting mixed up with the other. It's almost as if the two are synonymous, like two sides of the same coin.

I believe that this is both deliberate and telling and shows us that there was more to the Templars than just white knights in God's service. I believe it also shows us as discerning people that what the enemy created within the Knights Templar was not about to die or diminish in 1307, but that it sought to continue its system and false religion into a new age.

Remember, this is how principalities and their demonic structures operate. They create worldly systems that can be easily influenced and controlled from the top, but are supported by a structure created through beliefs and maintained by those willing to work within the structure knowingly or unknowingly.

Freemasonry is another prime example of this. Most of its members are likely well-intended, reasonable—perhaps even Christian—people who are simply part of a system that is counterfeit and influenced and controlled by a few at the top with unholy agendas.

The modern banking system likewise is a system that was created by the Templars to solve a problem, but has led to the creation of a worldly system that is easily controlled, influenced, and manipulated by a few for their own purposes.

While the Knights Templar will likely remain one of the most captivating and controversial organizations in history, it's safe to say that they were part of a much bigger system under the authority of the Queen of Heaven. Their establishment of the banking system and the control that they exerted through that system is something that is still being used to this very day to exert control and influence across the earth. Something that will continue until Kingdom-minded businesspeople arise and invade the banking mountain to displace those who sit atop the mountain and, in partnership with prophetic warriors, dethrone the principalities.

Personal Prayer

Father, I thank You for Your truth that sets me free. Jesus, thank You that by Your blood and through Your Name, I am forgiven, cleansed, and set free. Lord, I now confess and repent for myself and previous generations in my family bloodline concerning all involvement and engagement in or with the beliefs, worship, or practices of the Knights Templar.

I honor my earthly father and mother and all of my ancestors of flesh and blood, and of the spirit by adoption and godparents, but I utterly turn away from and renounce all their sins. I forgive all my ancestors for the effects of their sins on me and my children. I confess and renounce all of my own sins, known and unknown. I renounce and rebuke every spiritual power of darkness affecting me and my family, in the name of Jesus Christ.

I renounce all vows, covenants, promises, rituals, beliefs, and ceremonies of the Knights Templar. I specifically renounce all vows of poverty, chastity, chivalry, and all those found within the Latin Right and similar guiding documents of the Knights Templar that do not glorify You, the One True God.

In the Name of Jesus, I renounce and cut off from myself all literal, figurative, and allegorical meanings of all symbols of the Order of the Knights Templar. I declare that these symbols will not affect my life or the lives of my loved ones.

I renounce the teachings of Gnosticism and duality, which teaches that secret knowledge is required for salvation.

I renounce all false manifestations of the Holy Spirit and any attempts to mimic or copy or emulate the power of the Holy Spirit through natural means such as through sound and frequency.

I break off any connection, influence, or access to my finances and the Knights Templar and their beliefs and actions. I decree and declare my finances are rooted in and governed by the Kingdom of Heaven and not any earthly or worldly system. My source is Yahweh Jireh, who sees and provides for all of my needs.

Father, thank You for Your freedom. I rejoice that I am free and free indeed! Thank You, Lord, for purity, freedom, and victory in my life. Holy Spirit, in every place where my house has been swept clean, fill me up to overflowing. I welcome and declare purity and holiness in my thoughts, in my mind, in my emotions and desires. Lord, I declare that Your Word is alive in me. I ask for more of You in my life. Jesus, You are the Alpha, Omega, the Beginning and the End. You are the Magnificent One, the Holy One, the Redeemer of the World. You are Holy. All glory, power, and honor are due Your name, and I say that You are the Lord of lords and King of kings in my life. I rejoice in You, Lord!

Research Guidelines for Informed Intercession

It's time to delve into research for empowering your Kingdom assignments. In this time of Holy Spirit-led research, locate banks in your region that have Knights Templar roots. Locate the Masonic Lodges or York Rite Lodges in the region. As led by Holy Spirit, prayer-walk the areas where the banks and Masonic Lodges are located. Pray and intercede that the fire of Holy Spirit will begin to break through all deception, corruption, and demonic false presence through rituals performed in the initiation ceremonies. Prayer-walk the areas gripped by Knights Templar influence and welcome the Lord's glory to pierce through the darkness and bring revival, awakening, and transformation. Pray for those who are trapped in this dark bondage to have encounters with Jesus and to be radically saved and transformed.

1. Who were the foundational leaders of your region/ sphere of influence?

2. Were they Masons?

3. Is the Knights Templar degree a part of that lodge?

4. Is there a Knights Templar lodge in your region?

5. Are there occult groups who practice forms of Templar rituals?

6. Are there Masons or Knights Templar positioned or serving in government? Business? Education?

7. Are they using their money to fund movements or causes in your region?

8. In the earlier history of the region were the Knights Templar involved in expeditions?

9. Did they enslave First Nation peoples of your area?

10. What financial institutions are in your region/ spheres of influence?

11. Do they have Masonic/Knights Templar connections?

12. Is there homosexual activity in your region?

13. Is there financial corruption in financial institutions in your region/sphere of influence?

14. Have there been past moves of revival? If so, pray in agreement that those wells of revival will be awakened again.

15. How is the Lord moving now? Identify those areas and pray in agreement with the moves of His

Spirit. Intercede for more of His glorious presence, for revival and awakening.

16. Intercede for revival and awakening in the churches and spheres of culture and influence.

17. What are the prophetic and redemptive promises of the Lord?

18. What are His Kingdom strategies of stewardship of those words?

Chapter Ten

SANTA MUERTE

They will stand at a distance, terrified by her great torment. They will cry out, "How terrible, how terrible for you, O Babylon, you great city! In a single moment God's judgment came on you." ...The merchants of the world will weep and mourn for her, for there is no one left to buy their goods...and bodies—that is, human slaves (Revelation 18:10-11,13 NLT).

The border crisis we are currently facing is not only a legislative issue. It is a spiritual battle against ancient principalities operating through the drug cartel and demonic world influencers and corrupt government leaders who operate in pure evil and greed. As stated in the above scripture, two of the listed commodities sold in the commerce of the Babylonian Queen of Heaven structure are the bodies and souls of people. The Greek word for *bodies* in this scripture is *soma,* meaning "a physical body carrying the sense of slaves understood (collectively) as property, made of human bodies, to be traded or sold" (Strong's #G4983). Some translations, such as the New American Standard Bible, use this wording: "slaves and human lives." When looking up human lives, the Greek word for *human* is *athropos.* It means "a man, an individual, a body, a collective group of people or persons" (Strong's #G476). The word for *lives* is *psyche,* meaning the inner being and soul (Strong's #G6034). It is clear that the slavery and trafficking of bodies and souls is a key focus of this demonic structure. Again, this battle of drug and sex trafficking at our borders will not be won with pen and paper alone but will also require the dethroning of the demonic principalities thirsting after bloodshed, death, witchcraft, empowerment, and the perverse trafficking of bodies and souls. Allow me to share what we have learned.

HISTORY OF MEXICO

In July 2015, the Lord sent us on a teaching and prayer assignment to Mexico, such a beautiful land with beautiful people. We focused the first portion of the trip on teaching pastors and intercessors about strategic prayer. The second portion we engaged in strategic intercession at key locations of the ancient Maya and Aztec cultures. One key location was the famous Mayan ruins in Mexico commonly known as Chichén Itzá.

Before arriving, we prayed for the right tour guide who would have the insight to share key history. The Lord was faithful to connect us with the exact right person. Although not his real name, we will call him Mateo. He quickly informed us of his Mayan ancestry and also his active role as a shaman. It became apparent that he knew Mayan and Aztec history along with the history of the Spanish conquest and its impact on the modern culture of Mexico. He was like a walking encyclopedia! He taught us by taking us through all the periods and times of history. So I will also do the same in this chapter. The entrenched occult worship and death structures of the ancient demonic principalities and its ties to the current demonic manifestation of the principality, Santa Muerte, will be evident. A clear historical picture will explain the spiritual foundations and beliefs that became the open door of the brutality we see operating through the drug cartel. I will do my best to share without being too graphic. Some of this history is very dark and unpleasant. But rest assured that stories of breakthrough will be shared!

IX CHEL OF THE MAYA

Mateo delved into the Mayan culture and spiritual beliefs from ancient times. He was beyond knowledgeable in explaining the deities worshipped and their strong cultural impact. The Mayan pantheon included a multitude of demonic entities. We will briefly look at the most prominent ones. Itzamna was considered the supreme deity and was associated with creation, knowledge, and the heavens. Kukulkan, known as Quetzalcoatl in the Aztec pantheon, was known as the feathered serpent associated with wind, fertility, learning, and revered as a bringer of civilization. Chaak was the god of rain, thunder, and lightning.

According to longstanding archaeological tradition and also in accordance with Mateo's history lesson, we learned much about a principality called Ix Chel. This entity was one of the most significant of the ancient Mayan deities. Sometimes she was depicted as a beautiful young woman, but more often as an aged jaguar goddess of midwifery and medicine. She was known as the moon goddess of fertility, procreation, and death. In both manifestations, young and old, a live serpent was worn as the crown on her head. Ix Chel, along with other gods including Chaak and Kukulkan, required bloodletting and human sacrifice.

One method would be the throwing of a chosen victim into the Cenote—a deep, underground chamber, cave, or sinkhole made of limestone that fills with rain and water flowing from underground rivers. The Maya believed cenotes were a gateway to the underworld; therefore, to appease the gods sacrifices must be made. An article in *The Economist* reveals the following from recent studies.

> Between about 600 and 900 AD the Mayan inhabitants of the nearby city of Chichén Itzá, believing it to be a gateway to the underworld, filled the pool with sacrificial riches to the gods: gold, jade, incense, pottery—and people. Those victims, judging by their bones, were often young (half being under 18), and, though more often male than female, were well representative of both sexes.[1]

I will spare the gruesome details that the study of these bones revealed, but over half the victims were most often between the age of four and six years. Their deaths involved horrific rituals. The most sacred Cenote in the Yucatan is located in Chichén Itzá.

There was also the ritual of bloodletting to Ix Chel and other deities where one would pierce their own flesh and collect the blood to burn in rituals. This would be done in various methods that I will not belabor. There was also the removal of the heart of a live victim while being laid and held down upon a stone altar usually located within the temple or on top of a pyramid. Of course, upon the heart being forcefully removed by the priest, the victim instantly died. There was also the occasional decapitation. So evil!

THE AZTEC DEITIES

The Aztecs represent another ancient culture within America and Mesoamerica. It's noteworthy to mention that the Aztecs and Mayans weren't the initial civilizations in Mesoamerica. Historians point to the Toltec culture and Olmec civilizations as among the earliest inhabitants, both known for their involvement in human sacrifice rituals. However, the Aztecs distinguished themselves by taking the practice of sacrifice to an unparalleled scale that surpassed any previous civilization, as documented by early chroniclers. Some speculate that the extreme nature of these sacrifices might have been influenced by the Spaniards' harsh treatment of indigenous peoples. Nonetheless, historical evidence indicates that such rituals were ingrained in Aztec culture across their ancient territories in Mexico and North America.

The Aztecs, guided by their deity Huitzilopochtli, the sun god and god of war, departed from their homeland of Atzlan. This divine guidance led them to establish Tenochtitlan in 1325 AD, which later became the heart of the Aztec Empire, known today as Mexico City. Upon the construction of the Templo

Mayor, historians suggest that the Aztecs held a four-day dedication ceremony marked by human sacrifices. The exact number of sacrifices during this period remains a topic of scholarly debate. Some estimates range from as low as 10,000 to 20,000, while others propose figures as high as 80,000. Recorded history and archaeological findings suggest that the Aztec priests utilized four sacrificial altars for these ceremonies. However, some skeptics question the feasibility of sacrificing such a large number of individuals in the allotted time. The methods of sacrifice included horrific rituals such as heart extraction, decapitation, and forced immersion or drowning in sacred waters. These practices reflect a dark, evil, gruesome, and disturbing aspect of Aztec culture, characterized by its acceptance and even glorification of human sacrifice.

These sacrifices were viewed as a repayment for the sacrifices the gods themselves had made in creating the world and the sun. This idea of repayment was especially true regarding the myth of the reptilian monster *Cipactli,* also called *Tlaltecuhtli,* known as Earth Lord/Lady—another androgynous demonic principality, but most often referred to as Earth Lady. This earth goddess was associated with fertility and envisioned as a terrible toad monster. In the Aztec creation myth, her body was dismembered in order to give rise to the world as the fifth and final cosmos. For her to have been the source of life, it was thought necessary to constantly appease her with blood sacrifices, especially human hearts.

Quetzalcóatl, depicted as the plumed serpent, was one of the most highly revered in the Aztec culture as the god of winds and rain and the creator of the world and humanity. A mix of bird and rattlesnake, his name is a combination of the Nahuatl words *quetzal,* the emerald plumed bird, and *coatl,* the serpent. He was born from an androgynous god. Sacrifices were also done in appeasement to him.

Despite their involvement in human sacrifice, both the Aztecs and the Mayans possessed intricate rituals and beliefs surrounding death and the afterlife. Among these, a prominent aspect was the concept of multiple realms within the afterlife. According to their beliefs, the souls of the departed embarked on a complex journey through various realms, culminating in their arrival at the final resting place known as *Mictlan,* overseen by the deity Mictecacihuatl. To aid the souls on this journey, elaborate ceremonies, offerings, and festivals dedicated to the dead were held. One such event was the month-long celebration called *Miccailhuitontli,* also known as the little feast of the dead. Families would participate by making offerings of food, flowers, and symbolic items at home altars and grave sites. These offerings were intended to provide sustenance for the souls of the departed during their journey through the afterlife. This ancient tradition would later evolve into what is now known as the Day of the Dead celebration in Mexico.

SPANISH CONQUEST

In 1519, the Maya and the Aztec experienced a profound change when Hernán Cortés, a Spanish conquistador, arrived on the shores of Mexico with the intention of expanding the Spanish Empire and seizing the riches of the New World. Cortés and his expedition landed on the Yucatán Peninsula with a modest force of approximately 500 men. From the outset, Cortés encountered numerous obstacles, including hostile interactions with indigenous groups and resistance from Spanish officials who opposed his further advancement into the interior. Nonetheless, Cortés remained resolute in his determination to achieve conquest and glory.

As Cortés and his men journeyed further inland, they encountered the Totonac and the Tlaxcalans, indigenous peoples who would play pivotal roles as allies in the impending campaign against the Aztecs. Both the Totonac and the Tlaxcalans had long suffered under the rule of the Aztec Empire, and Cortés welcomed their support as allies in his endeavors.

In November, Cortés and his army arrived at the gates of Tenochtitlan, which was ruled by the mighty Montezuma II who was worshipped as a god himself. He engaged in human sacrifice and forced 150 women who were impregnated by him to abort their pregnancies. Despite being greatly outnumbered, Cortés employed a combination of military strategy, cunning diplomacy, and superior weaponry to gain the upper hand over the Aztec forces.

You see, Montezuma believed that Cortés was the embodiment of an ancient prophecy, which foretold the return of the god Quetzalcoatl. Consequently, he initially greeted the Spanish conquistador with enthusiasm, lavishing him with gifts. However, as Cortés' true intentions became evident through his violent incursions into Aztec territory, involving brutality and death, Montezuma's trust turned to hostility.

In the spring of 1520, tensions between the Spanish and the Aztecs reached a breaking point, leading to a violent clash known as the *Noche Triste*, or "Night of Sorrows." During this pivotal event, Cortés and his troops were driven out of Tenochtitlan, enduring significant losses. Despite this setback, Cortés regrouped his forces, rallied his indigenous allies, and orchestrated a daring counteroffensive. Following an extended siege, the city succumbed in August of 1521, signaling the end of Aztec supremacy and the dawn of Spanish dominance.

This conquest had profound consequences, bringing about the collapse of one of the most powerful empires in the Americas, and paved the way for Spanish colonization and the forced spread of Spanish Catholicism. Friends, here is where I could write another lengthy chapter. This moment in history not only brought the Spanish colonization, but along with it the demonic spirit of death of the Spanish Inquisition, meaning the forced conversion to Roman Catholicism and the worship of their Spanish version of the Queen of Heaven. This momentous period not only ushered in Spanish colonization but also introduced the oppressive influence of the Spanish Inquisition, leaving an indelible mark on the region's history and destiny.

We hold a deep affection for Spain and its people, cherishing lifelong friendships with esteemed leaders in the nation. Their time in history during the Inquisition is dark. Initiated in 1492 by Queen Isabella and King Ferdinand, guided by their confessor Torquemada, its demonic purpose was to establish a *sangre limpia*, a pure Spanish bloodline, and to eradicate heresy against the Catholic Church. This evil scheme led to the persecution and slaughter of Sephardic Jews, with historians estimating that approximately 800,000 individuals endured torture and gruesome deaths at the hands of inquisitors until its abolition in 1851. I have written and taught about this for many years; we have prayed extensively in Spain concerning this dark time and watched the Lord do a beautiful, glorious, and redemptive healing work.

LADY OF GUADALUPE

To maintain a neutral and concise stance on this historical account, it's important to present the events objectively. Nearly all historians acknowledge the significant role played by the Lady of Guadalupe in the conversion of indigenous people to Catholicism in Mexico.

On December 9, 1531, Juan Diego, an indigenous man of Aztec descent, reported encountering a supernatural apparition of Our Lady on Tepayac Hill. She requested the construction of a church in her honor. Juan relayed the message to Archbishop Juan de Zumárraga, a Castilian Catholic and inquisitor from Spain, who dismissed the request. However, subsequent appearances, including the miraculous blooming of Castilian roses (which were not native to Mexico) on Tepeyac hill, instructed by Our Lady to be presented to the Archbishop as a sign, led to a pivotal moment. When Juan opened his cloak to reveal the roses to Zumárraga, the supernatural image of Our Lady of Guadalupe was imprinted on the fabric of his tunic, widely regarded by many as a miraculous occurrence. Following years of research surrounding these appearances in many nations and having prayed at numerous apparition sites has caused our eyes of understanding to be opened to what some historians deem as explanatory regarding these events.

Prior to Guadalupe's alleged appearance in 1531, an Aztec goddess had been worshipped at the same site. The Aztec goddess's name, Tonantzin, means "Our Mother" in the Aztec language of Nahuatl, so some skeptics contend that the Spanish colonial church concocted the story of Guadalupe appearing to Juan Diego as a way to convert his fellow Aztecs and other indigenous groups to Christianity.[2]

In the late 1570s, Bernardino de Sahagún, a Franciscan historian condemned what he called the cult at Tepeyac. In his *General History of the Things of New Spain* also known *Florentine Codex,* he criticized the use of the name Tonantzin in referencing her as Our Lady.

At this place [Tepeyac], [the Indians] had a temple dedicated to the mother of the gods, whom they called Tonantzin, which means Our Mother. There they performed many sacrifices in honor of this goddess…And now that a church of Our Lady of Guadalupe is built there, they also called her Tonantzin, being motivated by those preachers who called Our Lady, the Mother of God, Tonantzin. While it is not known for certain where the beginning of Tonantzin may have originated, but this we know for certain, that, from its first usage, the word refers to the ancient Tonantzin. And it was viewed as something that should be remedied…It appears to be a Satanic invention to cloak idolatry under the confusion of this name, Tonantzin. And they now come to visit from very far away, as far away as before, which is also suspicious, because everywhere there are many churches of Our Lady and they do not go to them. They come from distant lands to this Tonantzin as in olden times.[3]

In the image and vestments of Our Lady of Guadalupe, elements such as colors, stars, and symbols already known to the indigenous people were incorporated reflecting a syncretism of their revered ancient deities, demonstrating a blending of religious traditions. Consequently, over the span of 500 years, many worshippers maintained the old precepts and understanding, inadvertently combining their reverence for Our Lady of Guadalupe with their traditional gods and goddesses. Absolutely, many truly love, honor, and worship our Heavenly Father and Jesus, and would not agree with and would completely denounce the beliefs in blood and human sacrifice and worship to the ancient deities as completely evil and satanic. For some, the spiritual door remained open causing a pull to be drawn back into the devotion and worship of death and the ancient bloodthirsty gods and goddesses, as will be seen in our discussion concerning Santa Muerte.

Mateo shared his perspective on this history with us. Individuals like himself, who align strongly with their Aztec or Mayan heritage, do not perceive the figure known as the Lady of Guadalupe in the same light as others. Rather, she is seen as a modern manifestation of their ancient Mother goddess, Ix Chel or Tonantzin. In his words: "I am a devotee of Ix Chel. When I find myself in a church where the Lady of Guadalupe is revered, I do not see her as that identity. To me, she is Ix Chel. Many share this view. Our ancestors had little to say in the worship of the idols and deities brought from Spain. Therefore, when we are in her presence, our devotion is directed to the goddess of our ancestors." Friends, this history lesson and Mateo's own telling of it were eye-opening. It is significant when the indigenous people share their belief involving history and also the syncretism of worship. Nonetheless, Our Lady of Guadalupe has become the third most visited shrine in the world. So let's continue in our discussion explaining the modern-day manifestation of Santa Muerte.

SANTA MUERTE

Santa Muerte, also known as Holy Death, the White Lady, and La Huesuda (the bony one), represents a dark saintly entity intricately connected with the essence and concept of death. In the aftermath of the conquest of the Aztec Empire, the veneration of death may have diminished or shifted into more covert devotion, yet it persisted, never fully extinguished.

> A 1797 document from the archives of the Inquisition titled "Concerning the Superstitions of Various Indians from the Town of San Luis de la Paz" mentions... the Chichimec people...who "at night gather in their chapel to drink peyote until they lose their minds... they whip Holy Crosses and also a figure of death that they call Santa Muerte, and they bind it with a wet rope threatening to whip and burn it if it does not perform a miracle."[4]

Another instance of syncretism between pre-Columbian and Christian beliefs surrounding death is evident in the celebration and traditions of Day of the Dead. The mixing of indigenous rituals with the Christian holidays of All Saints' Day on November 1 and All Souls' Day on November 2 paved the way to the contemporary celebration known as El Día de Los Muertos. Santa Muerte is the deity worshipped during these festivities. Men, women, and children flock to cemeteries to sing and pray for departed friends and family members and indulge in chocolate or candy shaped like skulls in honor of death.

Often portrayed as a female counterpart to the Grim Reaper, she wears a flowing robes, wielding a scythe, yet distinguished by her feminine adornments of jewelry, flowers, and sometimes cascading hair. There are times she is also adorned in a wedding gown. Despite some resemblances between Santa Muerte and the Grim Reaper, her worshippers believe they are separate entities. Whereas the Grim Reaper symbolizes death in Western folklore, Santa Muerte has achieved the accomplishment of emerging as a revered figure blending Catholicism, occult spiritualism, and indigenous influences into her worship. The Catholic influence of praying to saints and idols paved the way for those who are devotees of Santa Muerte, making the veneration to her an outflow of syncretism from the ancient Mayan and Aztec worship combined into Catholicism brought by the Spanish.

A brief overview of additional influences includes Santería and Brujería. In Santería, the Orishas, representing the deities or spirits of the Yoruba pantheon, are frequently merged with Catholic saints, as discussed by Anthony in Chapter Eight. On the other hand, Brujería, which translates to "witchcraft" or "sorcery" in Spanish, encompasses a wide range of folk magic and occult practices observed in Latin American cultures. In certain contexts, it has influenced believers of Santa Muerte, particularly within marginalized communities, where many partake in rituals or practices of Brujería. These practices involve offerings, prayers, candle rituals, the casting of spells. Both are very dark.

Most significantly, Santa Muerte emerged from history, tracing her origins to the sacred traditions of the ancient Aztecs and Mayans to whom death was not merely the end of life but a journey to the afterlife. They personified this concept in the form of skeletal figures. Santa Muerte, in her skeletal manifestation, echoes these ancient rituals. She is believed to be a product of *Mictecacihuatl*, the Aztec goddess of death, and carries forward the reverence and rituals of her predecessors. These skeletal figures were revered and worshipped with fervor. To the worshipper she embodied the hope for a safe and peaceful passage into the realm beyond. Such a demonic and evil deception.

Followers of Santa Muerte perceive her as a benevolent spirit, nurturing and protective, possessing dominion over death and decay. She is sought after in times of illness or addiction when devotees turn to her for healing and comfort. She is invoked for financial prosperity, legal matters, and safeguarding against evil forces by dispelling curses and evil energies. She is said to have divine wisdom and guides her followers toward deeper insights and creativity. Through her intercession, her believers claim they find peace and protection and a deep connection with the mysteries of death, mortality, and the power of the divine feminine.

Her influence brings the initiate in direct contact with the demonic, which opens the demonic portal of connecting with departed souls, demons, and enhancing magic abilities and practices. Her practitioners believe she fosters wisdom, strength, spiritual revelation, and empowerment, causing her to be favored among witches and magicians. They espouse her to be flexible in that she does not judge the reasons behind requests. Her devotees say she helps with positive, negative, evil, and fatal intentions, which has rightfully caused grave concern from civil authorities.

Two individuals have worked diligently at promoting the image of Santa Muerte in Mexico and beyond: Dona Queta and David Romo Guillén. They have brought hundreds of people to the fold and have made Santa Muerte a household name accessible to the people of Tepito who have been abandoned or rejected by the Catholic Church and the Mexican state. Her followers boldly claim that she does not judge their condition or actions and treats everyone equally. David Romo Guillén is her first self-proclaimed high priest. In 2012, he was sentenced to 66 years in prison for kidnapping and extortion.

In recent years, Santa Muerte has advanced her demonic agenda through the drug cartel and sex traffickers, leading the US Federal Bureau of Investigation to label her a narco-saint. This has occurred due to acts of violence and ritualistic activities on both sides of the US-Mexico border and, unfortunately, across all of North America and many Latin American countries. The cartels have formed cults around her, believing she can protect and assist them. Some have killed in her honor stating the tortures, killings, and death are sacrifices to her. Her statues are placed in graveyards, to be used in black magic and dark spells to bring satanic harm to people. While these criminals view her as a saint and many still profess Catholicism, the Catholic Church strongly opposes her, calling her a figure of evil and satan.

Understandably, law enforcement sees her presence at crime scenes as a foreboding sign due to the fact that drug and sex traffickers often become more dangerous when they believe she is their defender and protector. All of her devotees, criminal or noncriminal, proclaim her to be death itself. When these cartels utilize her as this symbol, it has a great impact and effect on the Mexican population and all the regions and countries in which she is now venerated. As I am writing this chapter, the following is a headline from a news article that came up on my notifications in the Daily Mail, "*Inside sinister Fort Worth human trafficking stash house where migrants were hidden in basement via secret tunnel and smugglers worshipped cartel saint Santa Muerte.*" The article goes onto to say this group has smuggled and trafficked individuals into Chicago, New York, and Georgia.[5]

These criminals depict her as being on their side. The result is demonic empowerment, creating a unity of cause. Their cause is death, murder, empowerment, perversion, and greed—causes for which they are willing to die. These cartels have impacted our nation and the nations and corrupt elite men, women, and governments across the nations who willingly ignore or empower their actions. Why? They too gain empowerment and great wealth. It is sad to report that the United States is the top consumer of the drugs being trafficked illegally into our country. And the United States is the top consumer of pornography and the prostitution and buying of those sex trafficked across our borders. At this time in history, the Mexican drug cartel is the number-one criminal threat in the United States and North America.

To me it is beyond comprehension that Santa Muerte's popularity has grown exponentially and is continuing to do so at an accelerated rate. I believe this goes without saying, but this is due to lack of government regulations on illegal immigration at our borders. Another factor is media reports linking her to drug cartels. This in turn causes an attraction of other criminals, gang members, and prostitutes to engage in her cult. She's become a pop culture icon, the favored demonic entity invoked in all forms of witchcraft practices. She is worshipped and venerated by many in the homosexual, lesbian, and transgender community. She has infiltrated Hollywood with appearances in popular television shows depicted as an inspiring character. Her followers now number approximately twelve million worldwide, making her one of the fastest-growing spiritual movements today.

OUR BREAKTHROUGH TESTIMONY!

Upon finishing our three-hour tour and history lesson with Mateo, it was time to pray. We made our way to the cenote where numerous young children had been thrown to the depths of the water as a sacrifice to the gods. We had a powerful time of identificational repentance and broke the spirit of death, abortion empowered through human sacrifice, and all occult empowerment to Ix Chel, Cipactli, and Santa Muerte. You see, the Lord was leading us to break this from the drug cartel and the border, but we also felt strongly to deal with the ancient demonic root of death and blood sacrifice empowering abortion in Mexico, the United States, and across all of North America.

We then went to the most ancient Mayan pyramid where sacrifices had been made. We climbed to the top and prayed. We knew that we had to break the spirit of death, witchcraft, and abortion and renounce and break the stronghold of these ancient entities across Mexico and the Americas. So again, we addressed, renounced, and broke the ancient roots of blood sacrifice to the Queen of Heaven principality and its agenda to kill and abort the next generation. It was another powerful time of intercession and worship on top of this ancient pyramid.

We made our way back to the van. We were processing and celebrating our time of intercession when suddenly one of our team members, Kate Larson, began to shout with excitement reading a news report. Within two hours after we prayed, the headlines became our confirmation that we had hit the mark. Reports were flooding across social media platforms and news networks of secretly recorded videos showing the admission of a corrupt scheme operating through Planned Parenthood—the harvesting and selling of organs from aborted babies in the black market. Planned Parenthood was being exposed and taking a significant hit in our nation and the nations. While this is one tangible result of breakthrough and we rejoice in this victory, there is still so much more to be done. It is time for the plundering, defeating, and dethroning of these principalities as stated by the prophet Isaiah.

"Come down, virgin daughter of Babylon, and sit in the dust. For your days of sitting on a throne have ended. O

daughter of Babylonia, never again will you be the lovely princess, tender and delicate. Take heavy millstones and grind flour. Remove your veil, and strip off your robe. Expose yourself to public view. You will be naked and burdened with shame. I will take vengeance against you without pity." Our Redeemer, whose name is the Lord of Heaven's Armies, is the Holy One of Israel (Isaiah 47:1-4 NLT).

BREWER TESTIMONY

The following is a powerful testimony from friends in Tennessee, Michael and Andrea Brewer. I want to express a word of wisdom. Not all are called to this level of spiritual warfare prayer. And there are rules of engagement to follow. This level of warfare is not to be entered into lightly. The Brewers have a long history of engaging in warfare through deliverance and have been leading and praying into their region for many years. Thus, they walk in the understanding and wisdom of when and how to address principalities. There are rules of engagement that must be followed. Again, great resources are *Authority to Tread, Glory Warfare, Discerning the Spirit Realm,* and our online Regional Transformation Spiritual Warfare School found on our website www.christianharvestintl.org.

Andrea and I had an extraordinary experience at the SPAN gathering in Texas in January 2024. Amidst the backdrop of ongoing challenges along the Mexico-United States border, where many were fervently praying, a vision unfolded within my spirit. While in prayer, I discerned a twisting serpent spirit swirling in the Rio Grande River, which marks the boundary between Mexico and the United States. It was clear to me that the drug cartels were utilizing couriers to transport narcotics across the river. This was a ritualistic baptism unto Santa Muerte, the deity associated with death.

In our region, we've been warring against addiction and overdose, stemming from the influx of drugs through cartel distribution networks originating in Mexico. This vision underscored the urgency of specifically targeting the spirit of death and its associations with Santa Muerte in our spiritual warfare efforts.

For years, we've been deeply engaged in ground-level spiritual warfare and casting out demons, but this revelation further propelled us into a realm of strategic-level spiritual warfare. During our time in Texas, Becca prophesied over Andrea and I, speaking of the forthcoming expansion and intensity of our monthly public deliverance services. She conveyed that what we had experienced thus far was merely a prelude to what lay ahead. Over the next six months, we were told to anticipate a significant outpouring from the Lord during these gatherings, culminating in a direct confrontation with Lilith, one of the ruling principalities in our region. This would be a spiritual showdown for the region.

Upon returning to Tennessee, during our first public deliverance night, I felt prompted to share the vision of the drug baptism under Santa Muerte and to actively break the grip of the spirit of death over our region. While we've always witnessed powerful displays of deliverance during these gatherings, the night we confronted the demon of death and Santa Muerte was remarkable. More individuals experienced deliverance from demons, and the time required for their deliverance was shorter than in previous services. The atmosphere itself had shifted due to the prophetic word and the faith that came with it. This facilitated an increase in the level of freedom as well as the power of our release during ministry.

This encounter activated a new level of targeted, strategic-level spiritual warfare and the transformative power of corporate intercession. We continue to remain steadfast in our commitment to confronting darkness with the light of God's truth, knowing that victory is assured. Jesus is greater, and God's power is stronger than any and every evil power operating within our region.

PETER AND DORIS WAGNER TESTIMONY

It is fitting that the final testimony of breakthrough involves Peter and Doris Wagner and Cindy Jacobs for their revival transformational work in Argentina in the early nineties. It was written by Peter telling the strategy of victory with tangible, measurable results. As a quick side note, this manifestation of Santa Muerte was San La Muerte and they referred to this demonic entity as male.

Resistencia, Argentina was the target of one of the first city-taking efforts in the 1990s, led by Ed Silvoso of Harvest Evangelism. My wife, Doris, and I, along with Cindy Jacobs and several others, joined Silvoso in a three-year effort to see a true spiritual breakthrough in Resistencia beginning in 1990.

The highest-ranking spirit in that Northern Argentina city of 400,000 was San La Muerte, literally translated, "St. Death." Thirteen shrines to St. Death throughout the city offered easy access for worship to the entire population. His idol was a skeleton. Why did people worship this spirit? Because he had promised them a "good death!" It is hard to imagine a people so hopeless and full of despair that the most they could hope for down the road was a good death! In fact, many had miniature idols of San La Muerte surgically implanted in parts of their bodies, such as under their nipples, so that wherever they went, San La Muerte would go with them and give them a good death.

The few Christian pastors of the city joined forces with Silvoso's team and declared war on San La Muerte and his cohorts. Open spiritual confrontation was the order of the day. Multiple strategic events took place in carefully planned sequence over a 36-month period. The culmination was to be a massive public evangelistic campaign, featuring all the leaders of the Argentine revival.

While the city was notoriously and openly idolatrous, it took some time to recognize the fact that a good bit of this idolatry had spilled over into the body of Christ as well. Many believers were found to be acting like the ancient children of Israel under Samuel—they had their modern counterparts to Israel's Baals and Ashtoreths somewhere on their persons or in their homes.

"Burn the Idols!"

Doris was preparing to travel to Argentina with Cindy Jacobs for the climactic evangelistic campaign. As she was reading Scripture the morning she was to leave, the Holy Spirit told her that in Resistencia they must burn the idols, like the magicians did in Ephesus. Ed Silvoso, Cindy Jacobs, and the Resistencia pastors agreed. So the evening before the evangelistic crusade, all the city's believers came together for prayer. The leaders explained how important it would be to do spiritual housecleaning in their homes before they came to the meeting. They began mentioning the kinds of material things that might be bringing honor to the spirits of darkness: pictures, statues, Catholic saints, Books of Mormon, pictures of former lovers, pornographic material, fetishes, drugs, Ouija boards, zodiac charms, good luck symbols, crystals for healing, amulets, talismans, tarot cards, witch dolls, voodoo items, love potions, books of magic, totem poles, certain pieces of jewelry, objects of Freemasonry, horoscopes, gargoyles, native art, foreign souvenirs, and what have you.

The believers agreed to obey God and to cleanse their homes, even if it meant giving up what might have been expensive items. They were to wrap each item in newspaper to protect privacy and then cast the objects into a 55-gallon drum set before the platform the following night. The drum was heaped to overflowing! They poured gasoline on it and set it on fire. This was a major power encounter, because the witches and warlocks had surrounded the area and done their occult sacrifices, killing animals, burning incense, and sending the most powerful curses they could muster toward the evangelists. When the flames shot up, a woman right behind Doris screamed and manifested a demon, which Doris immediately cast out!

The Fall of San La Muerte

Many unbelievers came to Christ that night, and each one was instructed to go home, do their spiritual housecleaning, and bring their objects to the bonfire the following night. As this went on, night after night, San La Muerte's power diminished. The breakthrough that the believers had prayed for occurred. Eighteen new churches sprang up, and the evangelical population increased greatly over the next few years.

As if to headline how the aggressive onslaught against idolatry had succeeded, God permitted a spectacular event to occur one week before the evangelistic campaign. Resistencia's high priestess of San La Muerte had been smoking in her bed. She fell asleep, and her bed caught fire. The only things that were consumed by fire were the bed, the woman, and her idol of San La Muerte located in the next room! No wonder the city was ready to hear the word of God!

Wow! What a powerful testimony. And friends, Christianity and the Church are still growing and thriving in Resistencia today. I believe the following scripture as declared through Isaiah is appropriate to share after reading this conquering and dethroning showdown in Argentina, "*Sit silently, and go into darkness, O daughter of the Chaldeans, for you will no longer be called The queen of kingdoms*" (Isaiah 47:5 NASB). It's time to pray.

Personal Prayer

Father, thank You for Your goodness. You are an awesome Abba Father who is always faithful to lead and direct me on the right path. Thank You for sending Your Son to die on the cross in my place. Jesus, thank You for the price You paid on the cross for my redemption. You are the Risen Lamb who defeated death and Hades. Holy Spirit, I welcome more of Your love, presence, power, and life as I pray this prayer of deliverance and freedom.

I say Santa Muerte is a demon perpetuating death and lies. And today is my day of freedom in my life from her and all areas of syncretism involving Catholicism, cult and occult practices, mysticism, spiritualism from modern forms to ancient meso-American cultures.

Jesus, I confess the worship and demonic activities of this deity that have been active in my family bloodline and my life. I repent for my own sins and ask You, Jesus, to forgive me and my past ancestors for any involvements, deals, and worship of Santa Muerte including the use of rosary beads, all practices of worship and prayers to her, and all dead saints on designated holy days, specifically All Saints' Day and the Day of the Dead and all connections with Our Lady of Guadalupe. I repent for the consumption of all forms of media focusing on and empowered by Santa Muerte and death. I repent for the buying, selling, and worshipping of her images and erection of statues, establishing altars, visiting her sacred places, and the use of magic as a form of resistance to laws of lands, governments, and as a vehicle to mobilize and control people by invoking and engaging her system of death, terror, and fear.

Forgive me for petitioning her, the rituals of evoking and invoking her power and favor in my life and others' in order to gain prosperity and good fortune, business success, justice (favor in trials), protection from evil, for demonic spiritual healings, to attract a lover or return a lost love, to dominate and overcome enemies, to curse or reverse curses toward others, use of amulets, oils, seeking revenge, making a vindictive request, seeking assurance of pathways to the afterlife, and the request for a painless death.

I repent for representing and being branded by her in tattoos, piercings, titles, and names given.

Jesus, forgive me for turning to Santa Muerte instead of to You. For seeking her occult advisors including sound and/or energy healers, as well as for operating in agreement and being initiated into Brujería practices.

I repent for involvement and exchanges by way of trafficking bodies, sex workers, drugs, illegal trade, murder, my offerings, prayers, hexes/vexes, magic and rituals, and all forms of sacrifice.

Jesus, forgive me for defying You by claiming my sexual orientation as my identity and image, along with all other forms of pride, rebellion, error, and whoredom that are working through or against me.

I denounce the positions of demonic and occult empowerments, energy, knowledge, and gains that came through Santa Muerte.

I renounce my agreements and covenants made with Santa Muerte through syncretism and use of ancient and modern spiritualism and all her imagery, including her image, robe, veil, draping of flags, reaper with a scythe, the crystal ball, skull, hourglass, terrestrial globe, roses, and the image of the owl.

I renounce being enslaved to bondage through drugs, guns, illegal dealings and crime, trafficking children or adults, commerce of the business of Santa Muerte, ritual patterns, shape-shifting, and its connection to animals.

I renounce the death structures and beliefs she encompassed through new age, Wicca, white/black/dark/folk/reversal/indigenous magic, and the death gods/goddess of Aztec and Mayan culture.

Jesus, by Your forgiveness and the authority of Your name, I now break off of my life and the lives of my descendants the power of Santa Muerte, including the names she is known by: The Lady of the Seven Powers, La Flaquita (the skinny one), La Niña Negra (the black girl), La Niña Blanca (the white girl), Señora de las Sombras (lady of the shadows/night), La Huesuda (bony lady), La Niña Bonita (the pretty girl), La Madrina (god mother), La Santisima Muerte (the most holy death), Good Death, Cute Girl, Little Mother, Virgin, and Key to All Life and Creation.

Santa Muerte, I remove your veil and robe from my life. In the name of Jesus, I now command the spirit of death to leave me. Death, I command you off my family and off of my descendants; your cycles and patterns are broken and no longer have any authority in my life. Praise You, Jesus! I ask You to come and heal the areas of my body, soul, and spirit that were affected and under torment. I invite You, Holy Spirit, to fill me with life, touching each area that experienced death, void, disease, mental/physical unrest, conflict, and chaos.

Jesus, how amazing is Your love! On my behalf, You died, took the keys of death and Hades, rose to life from the grave, and are now seated at the right hand of the Father far above all powers, dominion, and authority, interceding on my behalf.

I rejoice in You, Father, You rescued me from the authority of darkness and transferred me to the Kingdom of Your Son by His love, in whom I have redemption and forgiveness! I am a new creation who's being renewed in knowledge according to the image of the One who created the universe. I now accept Your love and take on my new image and identity as a chosen, beloved one. Jesus, You are the Truth, the Way, and Life!

Research Guidelines for Informed Intercession

As we move forward in guidance to assist in the direction of research, I believe it will be helpful to share that in recent finds across North America there are many archeological discoveries identifying ancient Aztec civilizations. For some this might be found in the history of the region or sphere of influence being researched. Remember, this is just a beginning guide. Always, seek Holy Spirit to guide in this process. Schedule times of glory-saturated worship and intercession as strategies of victory are being initiated. Pray that the cartel who are trafficking drugs, women, and children will be exposed and those enslaved will be set free. Prophetically declare the Word of the Lord, His glorious freedom, and righteous justice across the region and the people. As a prophetic watchman, seek Him for victorious strategies of freedom and redemption from His throne room presence. Intercede for the safety of those in law enforcement who are contending with the cartel. Pray for righteous governmental leaders and legislation to put an end to this border crisis and the cartel's demonic and evil schemes. Pray that all who are trapped in the dark worship of Santa Muerte will have radical encounters with Jesus and be saved.

1. Are there roots of indigenous worship in the region/sphere? If so, what worship was engaged in?

2. Are there ancestral burial mounds in the region?

3. Was there covenant breaking, bloodshed, and slavery by the Spanish, French, and early settlers in the region? If so, have those been repented of through identificational repentance?

4. Has restoration and restitution been made to the indigenous people groups?

5. Is there activity of Santa Muerte worship in the region/sphere of influence?

6. Is the region a known route for drug and sex traffickers?

7. Is there an area steeped in gang activity?

8. Is the Day of the Dead celebrated in your region?

9. Are Santa Muerte candles, statues, witchcraft objects sold in local stores?

10. Are there witchcraft covens in operation? Ones that invoke Santa Muerte?

11. What other forms of witchcraft and the occult are in operation?

12. Have there been past moves of revival? If so, pray in agreement that those wells of revival will be awakened again.

13. How is the Lord moving now? Identify those areas and pray in agreement with the moves of His Spirit. Intercede for more of His glorious presence, for revival and awakening.

14. Intercede for revival and awakening in the churches and spheres of influence and culture.

15. What are the prophetic and redemptive promises of the Lord?

16. What are His Kingdom strategies of stewardship of those words?

Chapter Eleven

CHECKMATE

Arise, shine; for your light has come, and the glory of the Lord has risen upon you. For behold, darkness will cover the earth and deep darkness the peoples; but the Lord will rise upon you and His glory will appear upon you. Nations will come to your light, and kings to the brightness of your rising. Lift up your eyes round about and see; they all gather together, they come to you. Your sons will come from afar, and your daughters will be carried in the arms. Then you will see and be radiant, and your heart will thrill and rejoice; because the abundance of the sea will be turned to you. The wealth of the nations will come to you (Isaiah 60:1-5 NASB).

What a beautiful prophetic promise! This is one of my favorite scriptures. I felt it important to begin this final chapter with the truth of His Word declaring forth His full intent to see His glory manifest in the nations. Habakkuk 2:14 also resounds with the promise and declaration of His glory, *"The earth shall be filled with the knowledge of the glory of the Lord"* (AMP). Friends, this is our Kingdom calling and mandate as His sons and daughters—to see principalities dethroned and His glory made known. We are more than conquerors in Christ to appropriate His victory over darkness.

I am also aware that we have been on an intense journey in this book! Truthfully, I could delve even further into identifying numerous manifestations of the Queen of Heaven that have enthroned themselves over nations such as Minerva, Venus, Quan Yin, Europa, Freya, Diana, Mazu, and many others. Through times of intercession and seeking the Lord as to what the focus should be in this teaching, He clearly led me to discuss the different manifestations of the Queen of Heaven that have been identified and taught. As evident in the testimonies, several have been the focus of the more recent strategic assignments that I and those within our prayer network, Strategic Prayer Apostolic Network, have been called to engage in. Another strong determining factor has been the manifestations of this entity that are active and overplaying its hand in society, culture, spheres of influence, and governments. This overplaying is a telling sign of the times we are in. When principalities are raging in the nations they are in essence exposing themselves and doing so to their own detriment. Why? Because those who have eyes to see and discern and ears to hear will rise up as the valiant army to see these evil spirits overthrown and revival and awakening stirred and captured in the hearts of the people, the Church, spheres of influence, and lands.

Therefore, to encourage, exhort, and to release a sending-out charge to advance as His army, the called and chosen ones, to conquer, I want to highlight a prophetic encounter and revelation that occurred in the early morning hours on September 20, 2020 while I was attending Head of the Year, an annual conference hosted at Glory of Zion by Chuck Pierce. Some of you reading will be familiar with the word.

> The enemy thinks he has secured great victories in this season, but I am the master of the chess board that the world, man and Satan have attempted to manipulate through humanism, demonic delay and antichrist agendas. I have sudden moves that Satan and corrupt men and structures will not see coming. There will be sudden moves initiated on the game board that will trump evil and corruption and secure victory. Remember, that while I hung on the cross, Satan thought he had won. But I secured the keys he had stolen and in a surprise, not yet seen move, I rose from the grave and defeated death and hell. Don't think darkness and evil have won. Their defeat and destruction were secured on the cross and sealed by My resurrection life. There will be more suddenly, surprise moves. I will initiate the final secure move of checkmate on the game board the enemy has set in motion among the people and nations. My Ekklesia must rise above the roar of chaos and see, perceive and discern from My victorious eternal throne room

position and operate in the victory strategy. The world looks different from the sight of victorious redemption. I then saw the U.S. in a vision and the Lord spoke, "Look for the next sudden and swift strategic maneuvers. They will come suddenly and swift but with great effectual victory." I saw the sound of the intercession, worship, strategic warfare decrees, prophetic proclamation and decrees resounding out in sound waves of the spiritual atmosphere. It penetrated and pierced through the canopy and shroud of darkness, evil, lies and corruption and glory, light and justice broke through shining throughout the land. Now is not the time to be silent! Now is the time for the armed and ready battalion of spiritual warriors to engage to secure the Kingdom order for the New Era. It is the now time to tip this reset moment into righteous kingdom alignment, time and harvest.[1]

Every time, I read this word I want to shout! Yes, a portion of this word does speak specifically about the United States. Praise God! We continue to press in, contend, and stand for the prophetic destiny of this nation and a great sweeping move of His Spirit, glory, and awakening. I also believe this word is a now word for the Body of Christ in the nations, as evident in the initial phrase of the word He spoke, "*I am the Master of the chessboard that the world, man, and satan have attempted to manipulate though humanism, demonic delay, and antichrist agendas.*" Then a further authoritative declaration:

I will initiate the final secure move of checkmate on the game board the enemy has set in motion among the people and nations. My Ekklesia must rise above the roar of chaos and see, perceive, and discern from My victorious eternal throne room position and operate in the victory strategy. The world looks different from the sight of victorious redemption.

Friends, I know nothing about chess. I have never played the game or studied anything about it. But the Lord nudged me to delve into the history of the game and to briefly share the big picture of what He is speaking concerning this *kairos*, strategic, time we are in.

THE HISTORY OF CHESS: A PROPHETIC PICTURE

Chess, also known as the Game of Kings, has undergone a rich and extensive evolution, drawing on many different cultural influences from around the world, with its origins speculated to trace back to ancient Ur, but with the more plausible foundational history being India in the sixth century. Among earlier influences is the Persian game of Shatranj, which thrived in what is now modern-day Iran. With the expansion of Arab conquests, this eventually made its way into Europe.

In the early period of Sanskrit chess, around 500–700 AD, capturing the king would swiftly end the game. The Persians, between 700 and 800 AD, introduced the concept of warning players when the king was threatened, known as announcing "check" in modern terms. This innovation was intended to prevent premature or accidental endings to the game. Subsequently, the Persians refined the rules further by prohibiting the placement or leaving of a king in a position of check. As a result, capturing the king became impossible, making checkmate the sole decisive method of concluding a game. So what does checkmate mean? This is what I discovered:

> The name Chess originates from Persia and it is an evolution of the Persian word for a King—Shah. The term "Shaah Maat" means that the King is dead. This was the term used in Persia for checkmate. When this terminology entered into European circles and then came to the English-speaking world, it evolved into the term checkmate. The current name chess derives from the word checkmate.[2]

The historical importance of checkmate reaches far beyond its linguistic origins. It reveals the strategic and intellectual core of chess, highlighting the necessity of foresight, tactics, and skillful maneuvering. The term accurately represents the ultimate goal of the game: to encircle and triumph over the opponent's king. As a game of wisdom and strategy it became used as a way of representing war and was even used for training and modeling warfare.

WHAT ABOUT THE QUEEN?

I then discovered the one who was considered the most formidable foe of the king on the chessboard. It is the queen. She stands tall as the most powerful and adaptable piece in the game. She possesses remarkable mobility, being the only piece on the board that can swiftly move any number of squares in any direction to attack or defend with great flexibility. In the hands of a skillful player, she is a formidable weapon. I find it very interesting that beyond its role in chess, the queen carries historical and symbolic weight. In medieval times, queens wielded power and influence, although some did with dangerous authority. This historical backdrop adds deeper understanding to the queen's portrayal on the chessboard.

The following discovery caused me to shout!

> Though it is a point of fact that the queen is the strongest player in the modern game of chess, this was not always the case. It was during the reign of Spain's Queen Isabella that the queen on the chessboard took up her current position as the strongest player in the game.
>
> Prior to this change in the late 15th century, when Isabella rose to become Europe's most powerful woman, the queen was only able to move a single square at a time. It was Isabella's rise to power that inspired the rule change that allowed for the queen to move in all directions.[3]

I had no idea about this fact until researching this book.

Friends, as declared out by many prophetic prayer warriors, "You just can't make this stuff up!" The first strategic warfare prayer assignment I led into the nation of Spain in 2004 was focused on tracing the historic steps of Queen Isabella and King Ferdinand in their demonic holocaust to annihilate the Jewish race through the Spanish Inquisition—done to force the worship of the Queen of Heaven.

The other emphasis was identificational repentance for the horrible treatment of the Native Americans at the hands of the

Spanish colonizers under the rule of Queen Isabella in the late 1400s and beyond. They were horribly subjected to slavery, abuse, violence, killings, and the forced kidnapping for the purpose of being sex slaves. Queen Isabella promised to protect Native Americans and completely allowed the atrocities to continue.

I want to take this moment and prophetically declare, "*This is the now time for the First Nations people. You are the key to the fullness of revival, awakening, and transformation in our land.*" As quoted by Billy Graham and Will Graham, Bill's grandson, "God is waking the Sleeping Giant, and I believe God will use you to bring the last great revival. This is a moment in history that can change our country forever."[4] Amen! We agree and set our faces like flint to see the fullness of the Frist Nations' destiny made manifest.

I was further surprised when research led me to the discovery of Scacchi and Caïssa and their influence that initially appeared on the scene in 1527 and perpetuated in 1763 in a poem written by Sir William Jones.

Scacchi is probably the first goddess of chess, but as the poem of Sir William Jones becomes more prominent, Caïssa starts to gain more attention. In the poem, the god of war, Mars, falls in love with the nymph Caïssa but she does not reciprocate his feelings. However, Mars continues to pursue Caïssa by seeking help from other gods, especially with Euphron, the god of sports and games.

Mars wanted to impress the nymph, so he asked Euphron to create the game of chess. He designed it with an elaborate chessboard and beautiful chess pieces for

Mars to give to Caïssa. And as soon as the god of war offers the chess set to Caïssa, he gets her attention by teaching her the game. At the end of the poem, Mars won the heart of Caïssa, but she won eternal flames.[5]

This goddess has continued to gain ground in the worldwide chess community. Some players, especially veterans, at times will be heard inviting Caïssa to be with them as they play. It is believed this will bring foresight and wisdom in the game to ensure a victory. Who would have known? I certainly did not.

However, with all the above being stated, it's essential to recognize that the queen's importance doesn't guarantee invincibility. Despite her considerable power, she remains susceptible to capture. Skilled players frequently strategize to entice the opponent's queen into precarious situations, aiming to exploit any weaknesses that may arise. The glorious truth is no matter how much value and power she wields on the board, the most valuable player on the board of chess is the King.

I am not saying that that those who play chess should no longer do so. That is absolutely not the point of this discussion. The significance of what is shared above is the prophetic picture of the revelation given, which speaks so clearly the message mapped out in this book. It is worth stating once more as the Lord spoke it to me. "*I am the Master of the chessboard that the world, man, and satan have attempted to manipulate through humanism, demonic delay, and antichrist agendas. I will initiate the final secure move of checkmate on the game board the enemy has set in motion among the people and nations.*"

COME UP HIGHER

> My Ekklesia must rise above the roar of chaos and see, perceive, and discern from My victorious eternal throne room position and operate in the victory strategy. The world looks different from the sight of victorious redemption.

This leads us back to where we began concerning the life and spiritual insight that is within the Book of Revelation revealing the invitation of the era we are in:

> *After this I looked, and behold, a door standing open in heaven! And the first voice which I had heard, like the sound of a [war] trumpet speaking with me, said, "Come up here, and I will show you what must take place after these things." At once I was in [special communication with] the Spirit; and behold, a throne stood in heaven, with One seated on the throne* (Revelation 4:1-2 AMP).

John had the power to receive by sight and he saw the door open to heaven. The Greek word for *door* is *thyra* meaning an entrance way, portal, gate, or door (Strong's #G2374). And friends, it was open. The voice he heard was making the sound and declaration of war. Within that war cry was a resounding invitation to "come up here." Some translations use the words "come up higher." The Greek word is *hode* meaning a position near the view of the speaker (Strong's #G6045). He was given the privilege to see what was to unfold.

It is significant to state the following: John was *in special communication with the Spirit*. He was in the throne room presence of His glory, Jesus, the most powerful and magnificent One seated on the throne—the right hand throne of authority. Many of you who have heard me teach and who have read *Glory Warfare* will be familiar with the following phrase, but I want to express it here as well. The greatest lovers make the greatest warriors because we have a cause to fight from and to fight for. We don't fight for victory but from victory with victory. And as Jesus spoke in the prophetic encounter, *"The world looks different from the sight of victorious redemption."*

You see, the more of the increase of His glory in us, the more of the increased glory in the land. The enemy hates this. He is a sore loser who has already lost, but he will not go quietly into the night. The more we arise and see from His victorious throne room position it causes a stirring up, an exposing of the enemy and his army of darkness. It's what we read in the Book of Acts. The apostles would turn regions upside down for the Kingdom of Heaven. Principalities of darkness exposed themselves by overplaying their hand. The outcome—their defeat through the victorious power and authority of the believers. They were men and women who encountered Him and His truth. Power is the capacity to do something and authority is the right to do it. In the encounter of His glory, power is awakened for the assignment. And obedience to Him in the assignment begets the authority to accomplish it. He not only has all authority, He bestows it to us. Rees Howells shares a powerful truth, "Man's extremity is God's opportunity."[6]

NOW IS THE TIME TO SECURE KINGDOM ORDER

> I saw the sound of the intercession, worship, strategic warfare decrees, prophetic proclamation and decrees resounding out in sound waves of the spiritual atmosphere. It penetrated and pierced through the canopy and shroud of darkness, evil, lies and corruption and glory, light and justice broke through shining throughout the land. Now is not the time to be silent! Now is the time for the armed and ready battalion of spiritual warriors to engage to secure the Kingdom order for the New Era. It is the now time to tip this reset moment into righteous kingdom alignment, time and harvest.

As we are nearing the close, I want to remind us once more of the message that was shared in Chapter Three. We are the called and chosen ones whose presence is requested with a purpose. There is a summoning to the army of valiant warriors to arise, engage, conquer, and dethrone. And as we do, this Queen of Heaven principality, also known as the whore of Babylon, will be thrown down.

Then a mighty angel picked up a boulder the size of a huge millstone. He threw it into the ocean and shouted, "Just like this, the great city Babylon will be thrown down with violence and will never be found again" (Revelation 18:21 NLT).

THE FAITHFUL AND TRUE KING

Friends, I believe we are in the beginning moment of the greatest revival and awakening in the history of the Church. I will always remember a poignant moment and conversation with Peter Wager. It was at a Wagner Leadership Institute graduation in 2007. As Peter and I casually spoke before the graduation ceremony began, he suddenly looked at me with an intent expression and passionately stated, "Oh darlin', what you and the generations alive in your lifetime are going to see and witness. You all will encounter and experience the greatest spiritual awakening in the history of the Church and Christianity. It will begin to break out in your lifetime. I will be cheering all of you on from the great cloud of witnesses." He then made his way to the platform to begin the graduation ceremony. That prophetic moment and Peter's confident words stirred my faith and instilled an expectancy in me about this great awakening move. I have carried a fire and passion of intercession to see this glorious moment sweep our nation and the nations.

In 2021, a group of us were in an extended time of intercession in the basement of our home. The Lord's shekinah glory was manifest. We were suddenly caught up in a "come up higher" moment. It was glorious and powerful. Three of us were in the same prophetic encounter with Jesus at the same time and could see each other in this divine moment. Jesus was standing in front of a beautiful wood table, looking at a map of the nations of the world. I walked to the table and stood next to Him. He continued to gaze on the map. Without looking up at me, He asked, "Do you see what I see? Do you hear what I hear?" I gazed at the map and saw His glory cloud of revival and awakening hovering over the nations of the world. It was as if the fullness of His glory filling the earth was going to occur at any moment. I responded, "Yes, Lord, I see Your glory. I see the awakening." His response shocked us as He asked a question we were not anticipating "Then ask Me what you want." Undone by His invitation, in an abandoned surrender we cried out for more of Him and for His awakening to sweep the nations. It was beautiful, glorious, and holy.

He continued to gaze at the map of the nations with His glory hovering over the nations. He then asked again, "Do you see what I see? Do you hear what I hear?" Through tears of awe and deep intercession I replied, "Yes, Lord, we see Your glory hovering over the nations." Again, He responded, "Then ask Me what you want." At that moment it was as if we knew He was inviting us to ask, see, and hear victorious warfare strategies in order to see satan's schemes of evil, corruption, and darkness defeated in specific assignments in the nations. We responded. "Jesus, show us the schemes of evil and corruption in the nations that You are assigning to us to conquer."

In that moment, He took us into another vision clearly showing us how antisemitism and anti-Christ principalities were stirring to manifest in the nations much like what was manifested in Hitler's time. I will not go into further detail about the fullness of what we saw and heard. But since this encounter, we have been in the process of engaging in the divinely revealed assignments. The first one was to Germany, which then led us to Berlin and the Ishtar gate in the Pergamon Museum as shared in Chapter Four—the assignment that resulted in the sinking and closure of the museum and the complete ending of worship to Ishtar and her demonic empowerment that was occurring at this ancient Babylonian gate. Friends, it is the time for glory warfare strategic assignments to conquer the Queen of Heaven and surrendered glory intercession to usher in this reset moment of revival, awakening, and transformation.

It is only fitting that our final attention and worship be turned and set to glorify the One who disarmed principalities and powers. The One who made a spectacle of satan and his army of darkness. The One who has triumphed. The One who is seated at the right hand of our Heavenly Father. The One who defeated death and the grave. The one who holds the key of David. The One who has all authority. The Great I Am. The One who sits on the throne above all rule, thrones, powers, and dominions. The King who is the master of the chessboard. And in the words He spoke to me in that encounter in September 2020, *"Don't think darkness and evil have won. There will be more suddenly, surprise moves. I will initiate the final secure move of checkmate.*

> *Then I saw heaven opened, and a white horse was standing there. Its rider was named Faithful and True, for he judges fairly and wages a righteous war. His eyes were like flames of fire, and on his head were many crowns. A name was written on him that no one understood except himself. He wore a robe dipped in blood, and his title was the Word of God. The armies of heaven, dressed in the finest of pure white linen, followed him on white horses. From his mouth came a sharp sword to strike down the*

nations. He will rule them with an iron rod. He will release the fierce wrath of God, the Almighty, like juice flowing from a winepress. On his robe at his thigh was written this title: King of all kings and Lord of all lords (Revelation 19:11-16 NLT).

And one called out to another, saying, "Holy, Holy, Holy is the Lord of hosts; the whole earth is filled with His glory" (Isaiah 6:3 AMP).

Notes

Introduction

1. Minnesota Art Museum, "First Free Saturday: Planterart
    .org/calendar/2023/free-first-saturday-plant-teachers, accessed
    February 26, 2024.
2. Spiritual Warfare online School, Christian Harvest
    International, www.christianharvestintl.org, https://span
    .teachable.com/p/home.

Chapter One

1. C. Peter Wagner, *Confronting the Queen of Heaven*
    (Colorado Springs, CO: Wagner Publications, 1998), 17.

2. Sandra Sweeney Silver, "The Meaning of 'Babylon,'" https://earlychurchhistory.org/politics/the-meaning-of-babylon, accessed April 11, 2024.

3. Publishers, *Ancient History Magazine* / Karwansaray, "Recreation of the Etemenanki in Babylon," *World History Encyclopedia*, January 21, 2020, https://www.worldhistory.org/image/11755/recreation-of-the-etemenanki-in-babylon, accessed February 26, 2024.

4. Melisaa Barker, "The Sacred Marriage Ritual of the Sumerians and the Kings that Practiced It," https://www.academia.edu/6101327/Sacred_Marriage_ritual, accessed February 28, 2024.

CHAPTER TWO

1. Gerhard Kittel, Gerhard Friedrich, and Geoffrey William Bromiley, *Theological Dictionary of the New Testament, Abridged in One Volume* (Grand Rapids, MI: W.B. Eerdmans, 1985), 196-197.

2. *Merriam-Webster's 11th Collegiate Dictionary*, s.v. "worry."

3. *HELPS Word-Studies*, 1987, 2011, s.v. "merimnao."

4. Kittel, Friedrich, Bromiley, *Theological Dictionary*, 1341.

5. Warren W. Wiersbe, *The Bible Exposition Commentary*, vol. 2 (Wheaton, IL: Victor Books, 1996), 578.

6. Ibid.

CHAPTER THREE

1. Gerhard Kittel, Gerhard Friedrich, and Geoffrey William Bromiley, *Theological Dictionary of the New Testament, Abridged in One Volume* (Grand Rapids, MI: W.B. Eerdmans, 1985), 429.

2. Johannes P. Louw and Eugene Albert Nida, *Greek–English Lexicon of the New Testament: Based on Semantic Domains* (New York: United Bible Societies, 1996), 423.

3. *Biblical, Theological, and Ecclesiastical Literature* (New York: Harper & Brothers, Publishers, 1891), 258.

CHAPTER FOUR

1. ETANA, "Hymn to Ishtar," https://etana.org/node/557, accessed March 3, 2024.

2. Wikipedia, "Inanna," https://en.wikipedia.org/wiki/Inanna, accessed March 3, 2024.

3. Ibid.

4. Wikipedia, "Sacred Prostitution," https://en.wikipedia.org/wiki/Sacred_prostitution, accessed March 4, 2024.

5. Johua J. Mark, "Nebuchadnezzar II," *World History Encyclopedia*, https://www.worldhistory.org/Nebuchadnezzar_II, accessed March 4, 2024.

6. Ilu-Asherah, Website of the Thule Temple, https://www.thuletempel.org/wb/index.php?title=Ilu-Aschera, accessed March 4, 2024.

7. Geoffrey Brooks, "The Curious Apparitions of Pagan Goddesses to the German Knights Templar," Ancient Origins, accessed March 4, 2024, ancient-origins.net.

8. Ibid.

9. Ibid.

10. Justin Tasolides, Cassie Semyon, Reen Diamante, and Spectrum News Staff Washington D.C., "House Passes Landmark Marriage Equality Bill Sending Measure to Biden's Desk," https://ny1.com/nyc/all-boroughs/politics/2022/12/08/bill-protecting-same-sex--interracial-unions-set-for-passage, accessed March 4, 2024.

11. Jasmine Aguilera, "Biden Just Signed Same-Sex Marriage Protections Into Law," *TIME*, https://time.com/6239672/house-passes-same-sex-marriage-protections, accessed March 4, 2024.

12. Michael B. Macdonald, *Goddesses in World Culture: American Goddess Modern Apotheosis*, Academia.edu, https://www.academia.edu/23776347/American_Goddess_A_Modern_Apotheosis, p.283, accessed March 5, 2024.

13. Scottish Rite Blog, "The Masonic Legacy of Lady Liberty," Scottish Rite Website, https://scottishritenmj.org/blog/freemasonry-statue-liberty, accessed March 7, 2024.

14. Martin G. Collis, "The Statue of Liberty," *Commentary: America's Goddess Part Two*, Sabbath Website, https://www.sabbath.org/index.cfm/library/commentary/id/3934/americas-goddess-part-two.htm, accessed March 15, 2024.

15. Selena Fox, "The Goddess of Freedom: From Libertas to Lady Liberty," Circle Sanctuary website, https://www.circlesanctuary.org/The-Goddess-of-Freedom, accessed March 20, 2024.

16. "Goddesses of Liberty," Coven Oldenwilde's Wiccan Website: Witches and Witchcraft in America, https://www.oldenwilde.org/oldenwilde/gen_info/pagan_us/goddesses_us.html, accessed April 29, 2024.

CHAPTER FIVE

1. "Lilith Through the Times: Demoness to Feminist Icon," Lilith through the Times, https://skhadka.sites.gettysburg.edu/Lilith/lilith-in-ancient-texts, accessed March 23, 2024
2. Raphael Patai, "Lilith," *The Journal of American Folklore* 77, no. 306 (1964): 295–314, https://doi.org/10.2307/537379.
3. S. Flannagan, "The True Story of the Hermetic Order of the Golden Dawn," Grunge, January 26, 2023, https://www.grunge.com/296071/the-true-story-of-the-hermetic-order-of-the-golden-dawn, accessed March 23, 2024.
4. Athena Long, "Lilith: From Myth to Feminist Icon," Legendary Ladies Hub, February 19, 2024. https://legendaryladieshub.com/lilith-from-myth-to-feminist-icon, accessed March 24, 2024.
5. Janet Howe Gaines, "Lilith," The BAS Library. https://library.biblicalarchaeology.org/article/lilith, accessed March 25, 2024.
6. George Grant, *Killer angel: A Biography of Planned Parenthood's Margaret Sanger* (Moscow, ID: Canon Press, 2022), Kindle loc. 12.
7. "Eugenics," *Encyclopædia Britannica*, March 1, 2024, https://www.britannica.com/science/eugenics-genetics, accessed March 25, 2024.

8. Kristan Hawkins, "Remove Statues of Margaret Sanger, Planned Parenthood Founder Tied to Eugenics and Racism," *USA Today*, July 23, 2020, https://www.usatoday.com/story/opinion/2020/07/23/racism-eugenics-margaret-sanger-deserves-no-honors-column/5480192002, accessed March 25, 2024.

9. "Tiller's license at stake as KSBHA launches new abortion investigation," *Christian Newswire*, http://www.christiannewswire.com/news/380004393.html, accessed May 6, 2024.

10. Ibid.

11. Cheryl Sullenger, "Operation Rescue's Top Ten Stories of 2009," December 3, 2009, https://www.operationrescue.org/archives/operation-rescues-top-ten-stories-of-2009, accessed May 6, 2024 .

CHAPTER SIX

1. Herbert B. Huffmon, "Obelisk," ed. Mark Allan Powell, *The HarperCollins Bible Dictionary (Revised and Updated)* (New York: HarperCollins, 2011), 714.

2. Douglas M. Messimer, "Masonic Stones in the Washington Monument," https://www.tuckahoelodge347.org/lodgeContent/nuggets_2015/08%20August%20-%20Masonic%20Stones%20in%20the%20Washington%20Monument.pdf, accessed March 31, 2024.

3. Ibid.

4.   Albert Pike, *Morals and Dogma* (1871), 850-852; qtd. in The Square and Compass, "Pike Quotes: Redeeming Pike One Post at a Time," https://pikequotes .wordpress.com/2016/02/07/the-square-and-compass-the -hermaphroditic-figure-is-the-symbol-of-the-double-nature -anciently-assigned-to-the-deity-as-generator-and-producer, accessed March 28, 2024.

5.   Moe Bedard, "The All-Seeing Eye: The Grand Architect of the Universe (T.G.A.O.T.U.)," Gnostic Warrior, June 18, 2022, https://www.gnosticwarrior.com/grand-architect.html, accessed March 31, 2024.

6.   Albert Pike, *Morals and Dogma*, Chapter XVIII: "Knight Rose Croix," https://sacred-texts.com/mas/md/md19.htm, accessed March 25, 2024.

7.   Albert Pike, *Morals and Dogma*, Chapter XXIV: "Prince of the Tabernacle," https://sacred-texts.com/mas/md/md25 .htm, accessed March 25, 2024.

8.   Jon and Jolene Hamill, *White House Watchmen: New Era Prayer Strategies to Shape the Future of Our Nation* (Shippensburg, PA: Destiny Image, Inc.), Kindle loc. 187.

9.   Cathy Burns, *The Hidden Secrets of the Eastern Star* (1995) 198; qtd. in Selwyn Stevens, *Signs and Symbols: Occult, Masonic, New Age and Cult Insignias and What They Mean* (Wellington, NZ: Jubilee Ministries, 1994), 99-100.

10. Alan Axelrod, *International Encyclopedia of Secret Societies and Fraternal Orders* (New York, NY: Facts on File, 1997), 61.

11. Theosophical Society, "A Priestess of Isis with Adam Warcup | Theosophical Classic 1991," https://www.youtube.com/watch?v=VRbfJAUDsck, accessed March 31, 2024.

12. Jessica A. Albrecht, *Eugenic Appropriations of the Goddess Isis: Reproduction and Racial Superiority in Theosophical Feminist Writings*, Orbis Litterarum, https://doi.org/10.1111/oli.12419, accessed April 2, 2024.

13. *Josephine Johnson*, Florence Farr: Bernard Shaw's "New Woman," (Rowman and Littlefield, 1975), 75.

CHAPTER SEVEN

1. Merrill Frederick Unger, et al., *The New Unger's Bible Dictionary* (Chicago: Moody Press, 1988).

2. Mary Fairchild, "What Does the Bible Say about Worshipping Asherah?" Learn Religions, November 28, 2022, https://www.learnreligions.com/asherah-in-the-bible-6824125, accessed March 29, 2024.

3. Ibid.

4. Ibid.

CHAPTER EIGHT

1. Amazon book summary for Mama Zogbé, *The Sibyls: The First Prophetess' of Mami (wata): The Theft of African Prophecy by the Catholic Church,* https://www.amazon.com/Sibyls-First-Prophetess-Mami-Wata/dp/0971624569.

CHAPTER NINE

1. *Super missus est* I, 7, PL 183, 59 D.

2.	See his letter, *Multiples et fécondes*, June 30, 1950.

3.	Rebecca Greenwood, *Glory Warfare: How the Presence of God Empowers You to Destroy the Works of Darkness* (Shippensburg, PA: Destiny Image, Inc.), Kindle loc. 83-88.

CHAPTER TEN

1.	"Who Did the Maya Sacrifice?" *The Economist*, https://www.economist.com/science-and-technology/2019/08/01/who-did-the-maya-sacrifice, accessed April 3, 2024.

2.	Andrew Chesnut, "10 Things To Know About the Virgin of Guadalupe," *America Magazine*, December 12, 2016, https://www.americamagazine.org/faith/2016/12/12/10-things-know-about-virgin-guadalupe.

3.	Bernardino de Sahagún, *Florentine Codex: Introduction and Indices*, Arthur J.O. Anderson and Charles Dibble, translators, (Salt Lake City: University of Utah Press, 1982), 90.

4.	Andrew Chesnut, *Devoted to Death: Santa Muerte, the Skeleton Saint* (New York, NY: Oxford University Press, 2012), 31.

5.	Maryann Martinez, "Inside sinister Fort Worth human trafficking stash house where migrants were hidden in basement via secret tunnel and smugglers worshipped cartel saint Santa Muerte," *The Daily Mail,* April 9, 2024, https://www.dailymail.co.uk/news/texas/article-13285181/amp/Inside-human-trafficking-stash-house-Texas-migrants-hidden-secret-tunnel-smugglers-worshiped-shrine-cartel-patron-saint.html.

CHAPTER ELEVEN

1. Rebecca Greenwood, "Check Mate," *Christian Harvest International,* May 21, 2021, https://christianharvestintl.org/check-mate.

2. Editorial Staff, "How Did Chess Get Its Name? (And Why Is Chess Called Chess)," *The Chess Journal,* September 25, 2021, https://www.chessjournal.com/how-did-chess-get-its-name, accessed April 9, 2024.

3. Editorial Staff, "20 Interesting Facts about the History of Chess," *The Chess Journal,* February 9, 2022, https://www.chessjournal.com/facts-about-the-history-of-chess, accessed April 10, 2024.

4. Erick Ogren, "The 'Sleeping Giant' Awakens," Billy Graham Evangelistic Association, May 7, 2022, https://billygraham.org/story/the-sleeping-giant-awakens-native-american-leaders-anticipate-revival, accessed April 10, 2024.

5. Editorial Staff, "Caïssa—Meet the Goddess of Chess (with Fun Facts)," *The Chess Journal,* February 14, 2022, https://www.chessjournal.com/caissa, accessed April 10, 2024.

6. Richard Maton, *Samuel, Son and Successor of Rees Howells: Director of the Bible College of Wales: A Biography* (Poole: ByFaith Media, 2016), 73.

ABOUT REBECCA GREENWOOD

Rebecca Greenwood, along with her husband Greg, are co-founders of Christian Harvest International and Strategic Prayer Apostolic Network (SPAN). She serves as an ordained minister and gifted intercessor, prophet, and teacher called to minister across generations to see the Body of Christ come into their Kingdom identity and purpose. She ministers nationally and internationally in seminars, conferences, and churches in which she teaches on numerous topics including prayer, intercession, spiritual warfare, spiritual mapping, deliverance, glory encounters, prophecy, personal and regional transformation, and the Kingdom of God. Over the past 34 years, Rebecca has ministered in and led prophetic prayer journeys to 48 countries and many cities and locations throughout the US, in which measurable breakthrough of transformation have been realized. Rebecca has been a guest on *TBN, It's Supernatural, God Knows,* and the *Harvest Show.* In 2020, she launched a new show, *Reigning in Life,* on ISN and a new online podcast, *Victorious Prophetic Warfare.* She has written for publications such as *Charisma, Pray! Magazine, Spirit-Led Woman, Baker Academic,* and is the author of 12 books. She graduated with a Doctorate of Practical Ministry from Wagner University, where she also serves as a core faculty member. Rebecca's favorite and most cherished times are making memories with the family on their Ranch in Elbert, CO.

Continue Your Journey to Spiritual Freedom Below:

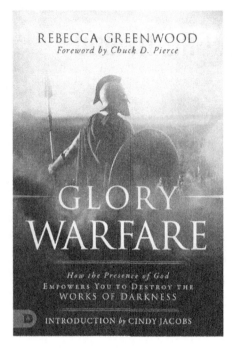

Glory Warfare offers a powerful revelation on waging spiritual warfare from the place of triumph, God's manifest presence.

Your handbook to discerning the invisible realm of angels, demons, and the move of God's Spirit.

Continue Your Journey to Spiritual Freedom Below:

This easy-to-use reference guide will equip you to identify common demonic strongholds so you can break them and walk in the freedom that is yours in Jesus!

Intercessors, prayer leaders, and pastors—and all who desire to see nations and peoples of the earth set free to hear the gospel—will find this a vital tool for breakthrough and transformation.

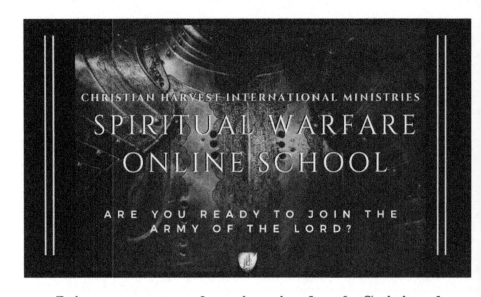

CHRISTIAN HARVEST INTERNATIONAL MINISTRIES

SPIRITUAL WARFARE ONLINE SCHOOL

ARE YOU READY TO JOIN THE ARMY OF THE LORD?

Join our comprehensive, in-depth Spiritual Warfare School that trains you how to hear prophetically from the Lord in order to receive His prayer strategies to decree and see breakthrough come to your region, community, and nation!

SCAN ME

Partner Mentoring

Christian Harvest INTERNATIONAL — Rebecca Greenwood

www.beccagreenwood.com/partners/mentoring

Find Your Identity.
Become a Kingdom Influencer.
Bring Spiritual & Social Transformation!

- Monthly Mentoring with Greg & Becca
- NEW Quarterly Teaching
- Access to ALL Live & Recorded Classes
- Access to Streaming Courses
- Copy of NEW Books once Published
- Partner Mentoring Community

SCAN ME

Check out
our **Destiny Image**
bestsellers page at
<u>destinyimage.com/bestsellers</u>

for cutting-edge,
prophetic messages
that will supernaturally
empower you and the
body of Christ.

Printed in Great Britain
by Amazon

52889634R00175